print, film,
new
media

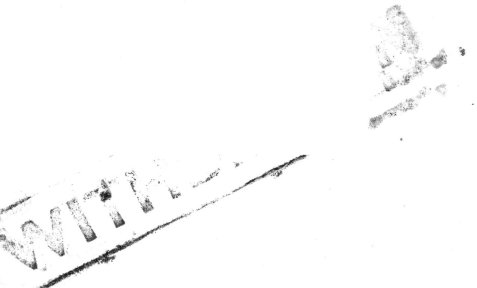

Foreword

Adrian Shaughnessy
Creative Director, Intro

As designers, we all preach the same message: we urge our clients to distinguish their products and services from those of their competitors by using the alchemy of modern design. We whisper seductively in their ears that we can help them attain the commercial nirvana of *separation*. We remind them that, in commerce, no quality is more desirable than separation. If you separate yourself from the crowd, we tell them, you'll get noticed!

Yet most creative work in the commercial arena – most visual communication – is endlessly formulaic and results not in diversity and variety, but in uniformity and standardization. It succeeds only in creating a vac-packed, freeze-dried, one-size-fits-all world, where everything looks the same. Why should this be? The answer, of course, is fear. Commercial fear.

This book is a record of our efforts to overcome 'the fear'. It's a sort of mid-term report – course-work handed in for evaluation – showing anyone who is interested in film, digital media or contemporary graphics that we've at least tried to avoid the anodyne, the bland and the formulaic.

It's not easy. We live in a world where risk is the new blasphemy. A world ruled by focus groups. A world where it's safer to blend in than to stand out. Where it's easier to follow than to lead. Where the easy money is in safety and caution. You can see evidence of this everywhere. You can see it in the clone-like repetitiveness of the nightly TV schedules; the uniform appearance of the magazines that fill the shelves in newsagents; the formulaic nature of packaging [what would happen if you *didn't* put tartan on a packet of shortbread?];

and in the commodification of pop music – a modern art form that was once rebellious, vital and dangerous, but which now resembles the artificial bleatings of genetically modified sheep.

But what happens if, as designers and creative people engaged in commercial work, we are paralyzed with fear and unable to do anything original or different or challenging? What are the likely consequences of this? Not much, perhaps. Except, of course, an ever-increasing homogenization of cultural production and a drab uniformity in daily life.

I recently caught a glimpse of this unwelcome future when I visited one of England's prettier country towns. People said I'd like it, that it was nice and had character. And if you live, as I do, in one of the world's great metropolises, it's comforting to think that there are places unspoilt by progress and rampant commerciality. I travelled there by train and went straight to a meeting in a dull office, with grey partitions and characterless furniture, just like the ones you find all over modern Britain. Afterwards, I was taken to the town centre and encouraged to walk about and enjoy the sights while I waited for my train. The town was pretty enough, but, at street level, the experience was blighted by the fact that so much of what I saw was numbingly familiar. It was as if I hadn't left home. All the shops were identical to the ones I passed every day on my way to work. They were all selling the same things. Everything was designed to the same architectural blueprint. It was sameness, sameness, sameness.

As a design company, a big part of our working life is spent trying to avoid 'sameness' – in other words, trying to convince our clients that in order to be different, it's not enough to say it. They really have to *want it*. Of course, after 13 years, we have many adventurous and far-thinking clients who choose to work with us because they know we'll help them to be different. But we encounter others who *think* they want to be different, yet, when it comes to the crunch, fear intervenes and they elect to play it safe.

We can't claim to have found a foolproof way round this problem – too often it gets the better of us and we end up with compromise. Yet occasionally, when the DNA is in place, we manage to produce work that stands out, work that doesn't get lost in anonymity, and, best of all, work that is successful – both artistically *and* commercially.

So, we're not the Baader-Meinhof of graphic design; we're not preaching anti-commercialism; we're not *No-Logo* hardliners, hurling shopping trolleys through store windows [although finding a photograph in a national newspaper of a rioter crashing through the window of a well-known fast-food chain during the London anti-capitalist riots of 2000, wearing a Primal Scream T-shirt we'd designed, was a proud moment – but that's as anti-establishment as we get]. Instead, we are fervent proponents of the maverick tendency in modern business. Our heroes are people who still believe in notions of personal risk, personal judgement and individuality.

We're helped in our thinking by a new force currently at work in contemporary life. It's hard to know what to call this phenomenon, but it's a sort of Zeitgeisty thing and it's connected to an emergent media-savvy generation who are wary [and weary] of attempts to manipulate them via advertising and marketing strategies, which are at best simplistic,

and at worst deceptive. It's also linked to the emergence of an educated postmodern generation, who are unimpressed with the old notions of authority and deference, who exhibit a sophisticated taste for irony and who, amongst many other things, live comfortably with the contemporary mix of art and media that flows through modern life.

I recently witnessed this mentality at work. Early in 2001, we were commissioned to design and write a communications campaign to promote a UK government education initiative aimed at 16–20 year-olds, called Key Skills [see page 140]. It was an unusual job for us, one that we were awarded because of our music industry experience. We were asked to 'market-test' our campaign. I pointed out, rather snootily, that we didn't normally do this, and that our intuition and street-level radar were usually sufficient. However, I was told that in the customer-centric climate of New Labour, market-testing was now the norm, and, accordingly, we presented our work to two groups of 16-year-olds [one from the north of England, the other from inner London]. The results were astonishing.

Without exception, these, admittedly bright, kids gravitated towards the more adventurous ideas. They disdainfully rejected anything that smacked of marketing, hype or window dressing. They dismissed smug copy lines. They zeroed in, Scud missile-style, on anything even mildly condescending. Their bullshit detectors picked up the faintest trace of waffle and subterfuge. And where we'd played it safe [not trusting our intuition and instead thinking of our client's expectations, rather than those of the intended audience], they unerringly pinpointed this. It was an instructive experience.

1 Angela McRobbie, *In the Culture Society: Art, Fashion and Popular Music.* Routledge, London, 1999.

2 The UK's supremacy in design and style was confirmed when the Ford Premier Automotive Group announced the setting up of a design studio in central London with 100 engineers. In an interview in *Wallpaper** [No. 36, March 2001], Wolfgang Reitzle, formerly of BMW and now head of Ford's luxury car group, said: 'London is the trend capital of the world.'

Most importantly, it confirmed our view that there is a vast audience with receptive minds who are resistant to patronizing and witless messages, who are capable of independent thought and judgement, and who have the ability to read the weather patterns in the mediascape. They also possess a sophisticated understanding of the mechanics of advertising: we *know* what it's all about, they seem to be saying.

This concurs with what the writer and academic Angela McRobbie seems to be saying in her insightful book, *In the Culture Society.*[1] She uses the term, 'the aestheticisation of everyday life' to describe a powerful undertow at work in current society. You don't need a cultural studies degree to know what she is talking about. Think of the following: the huge queues that formed to see *Apocalypse*, a recent show of contemporary art at London's Royal Academy; the success of Tate Modern [especially in light of the Millennium Dome's manifest failure]; the abundance of new design and photography books; the visual sophistication and narrative complexity of computer games; the UK's pre-eminence in fashion and style; and the popularity of websites offering visual pyrotechnics.

In the case of graphic design, there is a more prosaic reason for the new-found enthusiasm for this once invisible subject – the home computer. The ubiquity of this technological wonder toy has given millions of people an insight into the mysteries of typography, layout and image-manipulation – graphic design is no longer a mystery, it's something people do every day.

The UK's current Labour government were mocked for their attempts to promote the idea of 'Cool Britannia', but they realized that the creative industries generate a great deal of money for Britain, and moved quickly to acknowledge the contribution made by advertising, fashion, design, music and entertainment to the prosperity of the nation.[2]

Of course, all this seems to have gone unnoticed by the big design groups, most of whom have no interest in, or even cognisance of, the emergence of a media-literate, culture-hungry stratum of society. They've spent most of the past decade convincing big business that design is a business tool, something that can be applied like sandwich spread – glutinous and tasteless, and guaranteed to smother anything. I looked at the literature of one of the UK's top ten design companies the other day. Pages and pages about 'brand integrity', 'brand development' and 'brand guardianship'. Yet barely a mention of the word 'design'.

The problem with 'branding', as championed by the big design groups and the marketing experts, is that it is antithetical to the spirit of the age. Huge swathes of modern society do not want to be told what to think about *anything*, and, fundamentally, this is what most branding strategies seek to do. Current branding philosophies attempt to mediate our perception and understanding of 'products'. They attempt to prevent us from formulating our own opinions. Branding seems rooted in dubious notions of forming synthetic experience, manufacturing emotion and creating ersatz culture. The current vogue for 'brand experiences' is a depressing example of this daft trend.

[3] Comment made by Stephen Bayley in the article 'What's Your Favourite Brand?', *Graphics International* 82, 2001.

[4] Taken from a speech 'Beans and Pearls', given by Martin Sorrell, Group CEO, WPP, in London as part of the D&AD President's Lecture series. 2000.

[5] It is a safe bet to assume that many IT professionals conducted their early bedroom experiments into computer technology with Depeche Mode providing the soundtrack.

At Intro, use of the 'b' word is avoided. We tend not to use it. Mainly because the general public doesn't use it, but also because if you expose yourself to too much current 'brand theorizing', you instantly become locked into old-fashioned and restrictive patterns of thought and behaviour – patterns completely at odds with the times. As the writer and design critic Stephen Bayley, a waspish enemy of the dull thinking that surrounds branding, notes, '[branding] values derive from the product, not a flip chart.'[3]

This is not to say that all branding activities are dishonest, or that companies, organizations, institutions and a myriad other entities do not need to be 'made visible'. Of course they do. It is just that if we merely apply the latest precepts of branding, the results will almost certainly be vacuous and culturally moribund. The only sort of branding that will be acceptable in future is the branding of honesty.

Do we offer any sort of alternative? Is there an Intro 'philosophy'? Well, most of the time our 'philosophy' is no more sophisticated than the need to make a living, and nothing dispenses with 'philosophy' faster than the need to make a living. But I suppose we start with the conviction that *design is culture*. We're opposed to the sandwich-spread tendency in graphic design and we believe in radical, emphatic statements, rather than timid utterances. After all, even Martin Sorrell, the head of WPP, the conglomerate that owns many of the leading advertising agencies and design groups, has this to say: '…we face competition of another kind: from companies capable of generating ideas and designs and promotions and commercials at a speed and a cost far closer to that of newspapers and broadcasting than to the stately deliberations of conventional advertising agencies. At exactly the time when the traffic is getting faster and louder, and coming at us now from both directions, the middle of the road may prove an extremely uncomfortable place to find ourselves'.[4]

Much of the work you'll see in this book is record industry work, and perhaps the easiest way to pigeonhole us is to say that we're a sort of music design house that has stretched beyond the record industry. We certainly spend a lot of time talking to non-music businesses about applying some of the loose-limbed, freewheeling thinking that we do for record companies to the 'grown-up' world. And many are receptive.

Our music industry experience is a great calling card, and it's also a good icebreaker. I once sat with a group of hardcore IT professionals, talking to them about interface design, icon creation and the role of graphic design in the IT environment, yet all they wanted to talk about was Depeche Mode [see page 166].[5]

On another occasion, a few of us were presented to the project management team of a large organization who we were about to start working for. We were unexpectedly introduced as the people who 'do Robbie Williams'. At the time we did, in fact, 'do' Robbie Williams, but I was rather hoping we might be introduced as, say, skilled cross-media practitioners, with a craftsmen-like approach to design? But they were impressed that we'd produced a Robbie Williams campaign [see page 182], and it was thought to be an advantage when dealing with their project – a global graduate recruitment campaign [see page 048].

6 In the book *Reggae, 100 Essential CDs* [Rough Guide, 1999], authors Steve Barrow and Peter Dalton describe Dr Alimantado as 'one of the most original deejay stylists to emerge from the sound system scene of Kingston during the early 70s'.

So, devising fluid and expressive campaigns for companies and organizations, which might otherwise settle for inexpressive, monolithic design, is sort of what we're about. But to be a modern design company, it's not enough to be able to put ink on paper. You have to be able to hack your way through the media jungle. In other words, communication has gone supernova: it's a streaming data flow of messages and signs, and as a result, we make films – TV commercials, music videos and title sequences. We also design websites. We're technologists building databases and content management systems. We're project managers advising clients on cross-media opportunities. And occasionally, we get a hammer, rusty nails and some twisted wire, and we make sculptures for the covers of dub albums [see page 052].

In this foreword I've touched on some of the ideas that inform our work. Describing *what* we do has been left to the writer and design critic John O'Reilly [see page 008]. John is a perceptive and sometimes harsh critic of contemporary design. His commentaries on the current scene in *Eye: The International Review of Graphic Design* are sharp and to the point. We asked him to be sharp and to the point with us.

I'll end with a story. About a year ago, I looked up from my desk to see reggae guru Steve Barrow, long-time Intro friend and the person to whom this book is dedicated, standing before me. Next to him was a tall, handsome Jamaican. This striking figure was introduced as the great Dr Alimantado, one of the genuine heavyweights of Jamaican music.[6] His album *Best Dressed Chicken in Town* is one of the all-time reggae greats. I felt like a star-struck teenager.

I chatted to the great man for a while, before being dragged off to another part of the building for a meeting with one of our larger clients, a big, international financial institution. The Doctor left the building, only to return immediately with an armful of CDs from his car. Glimpsing me through a glazed partition, he burst into the room and, with a bravura display of generosity, typical of many great musicians, distributed copies of his latest album to everyone. The effect was as dramatic as it was unexpected, and the entire room was enchanted by this act of kindness.

This incident exemplifies the blending of business and culture that underpins much of what we do at Intro. It's what makes turning up for work in the morning worthwhile. It helps promote the feeling that we're something more than pawns in a game of financial chess. And it makes it a tiny bit easier to produce engaging work.

Audio Thinking

John O'Reilly

Album sleeves are masks. Not like one of those handy masks the characters peel away in *Mission Impossible* to reveal the person hidden underneath. Album sleeves are the contemporary equivalent of the much older technology of the primitive mask. The primitive masks of ancient societies had no value in themselves. It was only when worn that they had some significance, the person becoming a storyteller, a myth-maker, an actor. And this is for the most simple reason. The primitive mask, like the technology of the record sleeve, created an audience. By putting on a mask, you are 'putting on' an audience. The music, the band, the DJ become what they are when they inhabit the sleeve. They connect to an audience. But this isn't news. Anyone who has browsed in a record shop will tell you this.

If you've never bought a record just because you like the sleeve, you haven't truly tapped into the pop experience. One of the items on the great rock band checklist is having an instinctive understanding that what holds an album together, or gives a single impact, is what is communicated on the sleeve. Because of this, it would be easy to believe that sleeve design is an act of the translation – of a musical idea into the visual concept delivered on the sleeve. It isn't. Great sleeve design is the final edit, the last mix, the visual track laid onto the music.

Although, chronologically, the sleeve is designed after the music, smart musicians know that in a curious reversal of logic, the sleeve comes first. It is the equivalent of the preface or introduction of a book, written afterwards but read first. It's a navigation tool for processing musical data.

Take *Exterminator* [see page 068] for example. Before text messages, with their pared-down linguistic aesthetic, became the new language of mobile communication, Primal Scream's album of 2000 made typography a talking point for record buyers and journalists tracking the latest trends. This phenomenon was last seen a quarter of a century ago, when Roger Dean's inflatable *Yes* typography spawned a generation of pneumatic school copybook imitations.

As a typographic device, the removal of vowels and the stencilled gap lettering of *Exterminator* cue the buyer into the cover image. Faceless fighter pilots, supported by faceless ground crew, tool up, while the faceless Stealth aircraft, invisible to radar, swoops in. Emotionally, the cover effect of all these gaps is a kind of a dehumanized, freeze-dried chill. But that is nothing compared to the chill the conventional record company executive feels, who you can be sure will choke on his sushi. His logic is quite simple. Where's the name of the band? And how will buyers be able to read the album title?

This wasn't the first time a Primal Scream sleeve was created without obvious 'branding.' The sleeve of the band's *Star* single [see page 022], from the *Vanishing Point* [see page 018] album, consisted of two photos, back and front, of Black Panther activist Bobby Hutton, challenging the constitutional right to bear arms by posing outside a police station in Oakland, California, with a rifle. The name of the band and single are absent. At the insistence of the anxious record company, a peelable sticker was attached to the sleeve.

[1] Marshall McLuhan and Quentin Fiore, *The Medium is the Massage: An Inventory of Effects*, Penguin, 1967.

These sleeves seemingly ignore a basic law of marketing, which requires a product design to signal somewhere the name of the product being sold. But in neglecting a convention that, in any case, belongs to the 1950s advertising-by-numbers routine of Madison Avenue and is irrelevant to a sophisticated 21st-century consumer, these sleeve designs tap into a more elemental psychology. The apparently anonymous sleeves establish a relationship with the fan that is not simply one of seller and buyer, but is based on something far more potent – trust. In *The Medium is the Massage: An Inventory of Effects*,[1] Marshall McLuhan and Quentin Fiore call this relationship 'participation mystique'. 'Young people are looking for a formula for putting on the universe-participation mystique. They do not look for detached patterns – for ways of relating themselves to the world, à la nineteenth century.'

By doing away with the traditional signposting of the record cover, *Exterminator* and *Star* are powerful statements of trust in the imagination of the music fan. And, at a gut level, that's the first thing a record buyer sees when looking at these sleeves. These sleeves mainline directly into the fan's visual imagination. There's a levelling up on all sides, one of creativity. The band have taken a commercial risk, a gamble against prevailing packaging wisdom, and the record buyer gets to work on multiplying the connections between sleeve and music.

Great record sleeves such as these change the bleak, one-size-fits-all shopping experience into a genuine existential moment, where the curious music fan sees her own values and ideas recognized, validated and reflected back. Bad sleeves are a monologue addressed to the imaginary consumer of the marketing department that say 'buy me'. Great sleeves are the beginning of a conversation, of a romance, that starts with the cover and continues with the music inside.

The distressed collage of the *Exterminator* cover reflects the rough mix of garage rock plundered by the Primal Scream sound, which echoes MC5 and The Stooges. But *Exterminator* also explores the harsh, motorik European sounds of Neu and Can, and the cover mirrors this also. If our best-known posters of pilots and planes come from the pop art of Roy Lichtenstein, Intro has Europeanized Lichtenstein's candy-coloured vision by dipping into the Richard Hamilton toolbox. In fact, the helmet motif on *Exterminator* echoes the astronaut whose body is painted out in Richard Hamilton's 1962 painting *Towards a definitive statement on the coming trends in men's wear and accessories (a) Together let us explore the stars*. In the year 2000, the *Exterminator* collage suggests that military hardware is the new menswear.

The dizzying effect of the *Exterminator* cover is produced by a collision of technologies. The craft of the collage uses content with a digital feel, to the extent that there are patches of grey, pixilated blocks where a digital image seems to be breaking up. McLuhan talked about the process of old and new media colliding in terms of a cannibalism of media. In technological evolutions, each medium tries to eat the other. But what is the effect of this on the audience? Technology writer Douglas Rushkoff calls this dizzying effect a 'technology allergy', where the sensory apparatus tries to blend [unsuccessfully] two different representational formats. He's talking about films like *Gladiator* and

Star Wars: The Phantom Menace, where our brains register a gap between the computer-generated background and the characters on top.

This effect dovetails with the underlying message of Primal Scream's *Exterminator* – the music and the cover itself are about 'mediation', or how the world is represented and put together through media, whether that's the Gulf War via CNN or the media representation of a band who rechristened themselves PRML SCRM. In the flamboyant language of new-media business, the band disintermediated themselves of their vowels. To some, this may have been an artistic conceit. But ultimately, the condensed syntax lead to floods of publicity. The major consequence of the absence of letters was that the meaning was filled in by the press. The music and style press created headlines adopting the consonants-only style.

If the sleeve captured a cultural wave, it was partly because the aesthetic of techno-collision reflected the 'two-decades-in-one' feeling that existed in the 1990s – before and after the internet. Brian Eno talks about this clash of technologies and cultures as that between 'cut and mix' and 'click and cut'. There's a kind of media feedback as each is placed too close to the other, and you can hear this feedback on *Exterminator*. You can also see it in the video promoting the single, where US fighter planes fly through polygons [see page 132].

The video takes the design and art direction of the sleeve and delivers it as animation. It takes the post-Gulf War idea of contemporary warfare as a computer game and dramatizes it as a collage of found images. American footballers, motorcycle cops, fighter pilots, aircraft-carrier crew all line up against each other. War is a team game. But the video does more than simply mobilize the art direction of the sleeve. While the sleeve is about the collision of technologies, the video is about technologies of looking.

The artwork for *Kill All Hippies* by Primal Scream shows Intro going back to its Modernist influences. Soviet revolutionary film-maker Dziga Vertov wrote, 'We define the film object in these words: the montage 'I see'. The film-object is a finished étude of absolute vision, rendered exact and deepened by all existing optical instruments, principally by the movie camera experimenting in space and time. The field of vision is life; the material for montage construction, life; the sets, life; the actors, life.' The material for *Kill All Hippies* isn't life itself, but government and commercial film libraries. Because, ultimately, contemporary film-makers are closer to graphic desgners than they are to the traditional idea of the documentary film-maker. The key to the meaning of the *Kill All Hippies* video lies in the fact that none of the figures have eyes. Academics and journalists focused on the Gulf War as a TV war, as a video-game war. But despite the array of optical technologies employed by the military and the media during the conflict, its meaning wasn't about seeing. It was about the interminable analysis of images, from military press officers interpreting the meaning of pictures to *Newsnight* talking heads interpreting the meaning of the interpretation.

Reality isn't revealed through the eye looking through the camera, as early film-makers believed, and not even through the camera itself. Reality is revealed in the cut and paste of the keyboard.

In the edit. This doesn't mean that everything is now 'a simulation', as some commentators lazily suggest. It simply means that what is reality is more open to question than ever. We no longer have to take the world as it is, presented by big media.

You can see this idea being played out in the Robert Frank-inspired title sequence for *Witness*, a Channel 4 documentary series [see page 130]. In the 1950s, Robert Frank's photography book *The Americans* showed a side of this vast country that had never been seen before. Images of Americans that weren't glamorous or heroic, but spoke of the everyday passions and pain of people. In the introduction to the book, Jack Kerouac wrote that Frank 'sucked a sad poem right out of America onto film, taking rank among the tragic poets of the world'.

It seems strange praising a photographer who documented America for his poetry, rather than for his realism. But until the recent trend of reality TV emerged, documentary-making was always understood to be a narrative act, rather than objective voyeurism. The title sequence of the *Witness* programme emphasizes the idea that witnessing is an act of putting something together, constructing from scraps of memories and images. Glimpses of handwritten manuscripts communicate the idea of witnessing as a wholly subjective experience. Type flashes across the screen as if someone is creating a document of record, while the scratched film gives a sense of the layering of experience, of memories. There is no such thing as pure, objective memory. There are only bits of stories, stitched together. The point of bearing witness is not that someone is telling the truth, but that it allows them to make sense of things, to tell *their* story.

If the Primal Scream artwork produces Douglas Rushkoff's 'dizzying effect', it might be to do with the difference between Intro artwork in general and other album artwork, which relies more heavily on software. The same collage effect is used on Joanna MacGregor's *Outside In Pianist* CD [see page 159], which is more of a series of snapshots of a musician-in-progress, than a polished album. A musical score bleeds down the cover underneath panels containing the name of the artist and the album title. The label name appears in Univers over each side of the CD cover. Inside, the label name SoundCircus is sliced by the functionalism and, to avoid the clutter of text on the cover, the credits edge off the CD and continue on the sleeve underneath. In a gesture to modernism, the track titles are hidden behind the CD itself.

Joanna MacGregor is a classical musician and SoundCircus is her own label. Rather than following the 'smart-people-slumming-it' route of dying her hair orange and cultivating a working-class accent, she wants to contextualize classical music in contemporary culture by redefining it through record sleeves. If you don't believe in the impact of covers, that might sound trite. But MacGregor is gambling on the fact that the record sleeve has an integrity and slow-burning effect, which will ultimately deliver far more than conventional PR or marketing strategies for classical music that shout 'Really, I'm hip' or 'Honestly, the music is accessible'. The point of sleeves such as *Outside In Pianist* or *Perilous Night* isn't to reposition classical music as classic 'lite', but to resituate it honestly within challenging contemporary music such as Radiohead or Arab Strap.

The process of creating a successful album sleeve involves a close relationship with the musician. But the first thing a good design agency brings to the client is not professional competence. The most critical ability, on which everything else rests, is the possession of highly developed listening skills. And it's not listening in the conventional sense, but simply being able to follow through on instructions given by musicians. It's listening as interpretation. It's the listening skills required of an analyst – to pick up on what's unsaid, to make the link between what a musician is saying in a design office and what they are saying in the music studio on record with their music.

So, if there is a defining feature of Intro sleeves, it is the picturing of sound, of unconscious audio thinking. In a way, it's the difference between picturing the conscious image of the band and the unconscious revealed in the wires of the music. The most obvious examples of this are the Blood and Fire compilations. The obvious approach would be a bit of Jamaicana, rubbly Kingston streets and a splash of Rasta red, yellow and green. But the *Dub Gone Crazy* sleeve [see page 054] pictures a yellow, stencilled K underneath a crown [King Tubby's], painted over scratched, rusting, riveted metal. Behind the K, you can just make out a diagram of the recording equipment. The diagram is a key element because, more than anything else, dub is about electronic transformation. It's about tapping into the science of the mixing-desk.

You get a sense of dub's texture. It's a kind of negative layering. Unlike mainstream production, which is about building track upon track, adding sounds, vocals and strings, dub is defined by a process of stripping things away, breaking things down, musicians dropping out, until all that's left is a steely, resonant echo. Anyone who has shook and trembled beside a sound system knows that dub is music as pure, sonic matter. Which is why the sleeve of *Dub Gone Crazy* isn't the evocation of a place, like Kingston, or of a time.

There are solid reasons for avoiding particular geographies on album sleeves. Like the image of the band gazing into the distance, or wandering alone in an urban landscape, pop mythology is so imbued with geographic types that any sleeve drawing on a specific location doesn't risk cliché so much as importing a trunkful of cultural associations. The sleeve for trip-hop group Archive's *Londinium* [see page 152] was potentially a tourist guide waiting to happen. Red Buses. Black Cabs. Bright lights, big city. But the Archive cover turns geography into a series of co-ordinates – the city is divested of all its baggage. Location becomes the intersection of longitude and latitude. The cover of 1996's *Londinium* is a geological cross-section, at a time when technological evolution has meant that place has given way to cyberspace. The city, which provided the backdrop to the great political, social and cultural events and upheavals of the 20th century, has begun its slow downloading onto the network. The map of the city is being redrawn.

The *Londinium* cover pictures exactly the mood that was expressed in trip-hop's take on mid-1990s Britain. The paranoia that ripples through the surface of the trip-hop sound wasn't an effect of too much weed. It was the expression of a fear of dislocation, of being unable to locate yourself in the strange spaces being created by technologies such

2 Thomas Hine,
The Total Package.
Little, Brown and Company, 1995.

as CCTV and the increasingly popular technology of the internet. This paranoia produced a fascination with tracking devices and mapping.

The sense of dislocated romance you hear in Archive's sultry trip-hop sound is heightened by the cover and the images inside. The imaginary permanence of human love is made even more bitter-sweet, not just by geographic co-ordinates, but by the dating of each image. *Londinium* pictures a moment where the architecture of the city – the overground – went underground. And the underground – the networks – went overground.

Equally, for a band like Stereolab, the issue of sleeve design becomes one of furnishing an image-sound, rather than presenting a defining image of the band. And more than most bands, Stereolab sleeves are integral to what they do. Alongside their musical audio-stream, throughout the 1990s Stereolab educated their audience in a parallel visual-stream. The band's name evokes impersonality, riffing off images of science – boffins in lab coats, beavering away at musical experimentation. But Stereolab are The Beach Boys by the Seine, Kraftwerk on surfboards. They are purveyors of avant-pop. There's a child-like utopianism about their idea of a scientific solution to pop.

Like their name, which mixes the impersonal with the vital, Stereolab's music is also paradoxical. The dirge and drone of Krautrock is allied to a fizzing pop minimalism. A dub album is about sonorousness and deep textures. But the Stereolab sound is all bright surfaces and Euro-cool vocal harmonies. The Intro cover for *Aluminum Tunes* [see page 164] sets the name of band and album in dramatic relief.

The typography is a kind of modernist variation on the *Hollywood* lettering that overlooks La-La Land, evoking the cinematic quality of their music. Its 3-D extruded appearance reflects the utopian aspect of Stereolab, feeding the idea of the band's musical project as heroic endeavour. When you open the sleeve, the typography of each song title is set in its own skewed perspective, like the film titles on the front of a cinema. And if each title floats independently on the sleeve, that's because this isn't a new album, but a collection of unreleased and rare recordings.

Stereolab have been around for about ten years. So it's surprising that, for a band deeply wedded to an aesthetic of impersonality, it wasn't until the Intro cover for *Dots and Loops* [see page 162] that the clear lines of their modernist pop began to be reflected in the cover. The simple two-colour sleeve of *Dots and Loops* establishes a visual template to match the serialism of their music. Likewise, the two colour-sleeve of their follow-up album *Cobra and Phases Group Play Voltage In The Milky Night* [see page 165] begins to establish a recognizable Stereolab sleeve aesthetic. The modulation of the Stereolab synthesizer sounds are pictured on these sleeves through simple variations in typography, rather than through an image. In the 1930s, marketing psychologist Louis Cheskin named this phenomenon 'sensation transference',[2] where the visual elements of package design transform one sensory experience into another. Just as the dreamy Stereolab bubble of sound balloons through your stereo, so the typography of *Cobra and Phases* swims on the page over undulating waves. What the Archive and Stereolab covers have in common is a sense of pure surface, reflecting the sonic drift of their music.

The innovation of the *Dub Gone Crazy*, Archive and Stereolab sleeves lies partly in the way they remix powerful mythologies – of reggae, of London and of retro. A much harder task is the way in which the sleeves of Barry Adamson, Broadcast and Luke Slater take on the collective mythology of cinema.

The most striking allusion to the cinematic medium is Broadcast's *The Noise Made by People* [see page 078]. The sleeve becomes the title sequence of a movie as the chunky, brutalist Saul Bass-like typography solidifies the sleeve image. Members of the band are pictured inside the letters – characters of the Broadcast 'film'. *The Noise Made by People* is a jagged, angular take on rollneck-sweater 1960s pop. When you open the CD, the cracked concrete effect of the cover materializes as the sleeve and cover separate. The lyrics and images for the 12 tracks are on three separate cards, each resembling a detail from a film poster.

The disconnectedness of the inner sleeve, its incompleteness, the fact it's not quite whole, isn't a designer's whim. It is directly linked to the dynamic of melancholy that is at the heart of Broadcast's music. Musically, Broadcast's sad tone inhabits the flat vocals of Trish Keenan, the minor key in which the songs are composed and the restless sonic detours, which promise to take you somewhere before drifting away. This melancholy is pictured on the sleeve itself, in the images of the band in the lettering, where each cropped facial shot captures them in a private moment of reflection or gazing into the distance, looking for some promise of completion that will never arrive.

The sleeve of Luke Slater's electronic breakbeat album *Wireless* [see page 042] pictures stills from an imaginary crime drama. This is more than simply a musician playing out some teenage film-star fantasy. The cover depicts a crouching, bloody-nosed character, staring up at someone in a coat. An extract from a novel or script appears at the bottom of the image: 'I strained my ears to listen to the conversation as the tape reeled on insanely – radio tuned to a dead station. Outside the Sunbeam started up – another click, a sharp hiss, bone on concrete.' The point is made. What does the DJ/electronic musician do? He listens, he samples. This isn't any old crime mythology. It's the DJ as Coppola's Harry Caul from *The Conversation* or Jack Terry from *Blow Out*. It's the sampler as voyeur.

Inside the sleeve, the narrative moves on, with each opening of the sleeve divided into four panels. It's the sleeve as storyboard. As the narrative unfolds in an apartment, cropped images show details from listening technologies – entryphone, reel-to-reel, music tape and gaffer tape. You close the booklet and see the DJ desperately listening to his reel-to reel, as the bandaged finger of his tormentor appears. It's himself.

Similarly, musician Barry Adamson has made a career out of chasing himself down on record, using his music to explore and unpack his psychobiography. A child of mixed-race parents, Adamson's music has always been fuelled by issues of belonging, of being caught in the middle of two cultures. Adamson always puts his id out on display. Whether it's in the punning vocabulary of his lyrics or song titles, such as *Deja Voodoo* on *As Above So Below* [see page 114] or in the imaginary film soundtracks he creates

[3] William Hollingsworth Whyte, *The Organization Man*. Simon & Schuster, 1956.

in his music. *As Above So Below* places Adamson in a series of shadowy scenarios; *What it Means*: the dragnet is out, Barry is on the run from existential dread, chased by driving bass and ominous, low-key, synthesizer sirens; *Come Hell or High Water*: Barry, accompanied by vibes and piano, is condemned to life with a broken heart, without remission or parole; *Still I Rise*: Barry is the fallen angel in southern-preacher mode, bearing witness to human defiance.

The album, like all his work, is about being caught in the middle, between American and European idioms – of jazz, the cinema, psychoanalysis – and the place where all these figures meet is a French word describing an American genre – the dreamworld of noir.

The title of the album is reflected in the double image on the cover, with Adamson the blurred figure on top. Below, there's an image of a zebra-crossing, shot in German Expressionist style, evoking the window blinds motif in film noir. The inner sleeve plays out the drama of light and darkness, with lush shadowy lamps, and the noir architecture of the spiral staircase. Finally, there's the pay-off of the escape route – so close you can touch it – pictured in the closing image of a station platform number.

The Adamson cover and its noir-ish allusion provides a way into the Intro design gene. In the history of 20th-century American culture, film noir was a transitional culture. It was a genre baptized after the event by French film-makers and critics, while noir's content itself played out another French philosophy – existentialism. This practical philosophy of living argued that you are the author of your own actions, the creator of your own value system.

It wasn't until the 1950s, in the work of authors such as Norman Mailer and Jack Kerouac, artists such as Jackson Pollock and Wallace Berman, photographers like Robert Frank and, most significantly, with the emergence of rock'n'roll, that a uniquely American Existentialism emerged. It was a unique idiom that found an audience in a culture immersed in the corporate philosophy of consensus, famously characterized by William Hollingsworth Whyte in *The Organization Man*.[3]

And it's this existentialism that is played out in the soul of pop, in bands and DJs alone in scuzzy rehearsal rooms, in bedrooms, spending dole money on second-hand equipment, risking health and sanity to make music that has no audience as yet, only because they are driven by an irrational belief in their own creativity.

The casual viewer of an Intro sleeve may see Intro's modernist instincts in its clean design, its use of collage, its rational ordering of information even in its fonts. But while this may have been the taste of the designers, a responsive, interested agency will always be transformed by the work it does for its clients. And the result, in Intro's case, of their work for the music industry has been this grafting of American Existentialism onto European Modernism. In Britain's current print culture, content is not so much wedded to 'modernist' design as handcuffed to it. The aesthetic of 'clean' design of newspapers and magazines wipes away all traces of self-expression. It's the modernism that's often criticized as being Modernism, without its founding ethics or ideology. The Intro style is one escape route from the hi-tech prison aesthetic of what passes for modernism.

The best example of this is the Depeche Mode collection *The Singles 86>98* [see page 166]. The sleeve design for any compilation album is a problem. The design cues aren't coming from one specific concept, which a band are toying around with at one moment in time, as they do when creating an album. Even more difficult for the designer is cueing in the nuances of Depeche Mode's career curve. 1986 marks the year when the band gave their synth-pop a more experimental and darker turn. In the period 1986–1996, the band plummeted the depths of heroin addiction and leather skirts, while delivering shiny, hi-tech despair, sexual seediness draped in the language of religious dementia. Imagine Prince living and recording an album in Berlin, while reading *Venus In Furs*. No other pop band has mined the depths of modernist alienation with such purity or bleakness, while managing to shift vast quantities of records.

All of this is condensed in the choice of a simple technology. The bands initials and album are on LED displays, which were then photographed in landscapes, highways, cinemas, train stations – dm 86–98. The LED has a kind of modernist retro feel to it, analogue nostalgia which harks back to the band's origins in the emergence of cheap synthesizer technology. And, of course, the band name and album title in white dot matrix print has that 1980s electronic billboard feel to it.

The LED displays, equidistant and in perfect regimented order in front of blue skies, desert, and mountains, are a classical modernist sign of technology triumphing over nature. They dominate the frame. While the series of different locations gives the album an open-topped, road-movie feel to

it, along with the detail of Highway 101 inside the sleeve, which also alludes to their 101 album.

And it's this sense of space that gives design companies with modernist instincts an edge in web design. For despite our preoccupation with broadband, with faster processors, the only reason we are obsessed with internet speed is because it gives us a more elaborate sense of space on the net and in computer games.

Whether the Depeche Mode sleeve is Intro's best work is a matter of taste. But it is possibly their most emblematic. It's a Michael Mann moment, and if Intro were a film director they'd be Michael Mann. Just as films like *Manhunter* and *Heat* locate defining existential moments in the heroic, modernist landscapes of the skyscraper, the city, the airport, in modernist houses overlooking the ocean, so Intro works inject a sense of time into their modernist preoccupation with space. And this comes from working with rock musicians. Because deep down in the struggle for survival and recognition, DJs and bands see their work as a matter of destiny.

But if businesses like Deutsche Bank have come knocking at Intro's door for a recruitment catalogue, it's not necessarily because they want to fill their asset management department with Depeche Mode fans. Jacques Attali, French economist and adviser to President Mitterand in the 1980s and founding President of the European Bank for Reconstruction, argued that 'music is prophecy'. The thought that music is prophecy is based on the idea that changes in music technology and the economic organization of music has always been a template for wider social changes. 'Music's styles and

[4] Jacques Attali,
Noise: The Political Economy of Music,
translated by Brian Massumi.
University of Minnesota Press, 1985.

economic organization are ahead of the rest of society because it explores, much faster than material reality can, the entire range of possibilities in a given code. It makes audible the new world that will gradually become visible, that will impose itself and regulate the order of things; it is not only the image of things, but the transcending of the everyday, the herald of the future.'[4] Attali's argument that music is the prototype for the wider economy is illustrated by the copyright issues stemming from sampling technologies in the 1980s, and, more recently, the effects of Napster on music distribution.

The pages of Deutsche Bank's Graduate Recruitment brochure [see page 048] divide up into image scenarios and narratives from current employees. The images are aspirational, selling the idea that graduates applying to the firm will find themselves in a dynamic metropolis, in a hi-tech skyscraper overlooking Manhattan, looking out onto a Singapore street from their apartment. Whether those recruited to Deutsche Bank will have their expectations met is not the issue. The use of landscape format gives the pictorials a wide-screen feel. But, unlike previous generations, who would have been sold security and stability, what Deutsche Bank is selling is not corporate comfort, but a kind of existential challenge. And it's this atmosphere that Deutsche Bank is buying. They are selling an ethic rather than a brand. This is what distinguishes Intro from other design agencies, who have turned themselves into 'brand' consultants. What branding agencies have done is to brand the idea of branding, and, in effect, they are selling a lottery ticket to companies desperate enough to believe a change of logo or image will transform their business.

The idea of branding is the last gasp of the pre-digital age. Marshall McLuhan pointed out that, initially, the content of a new medium is an old medium. It's the same with thinking. Branding consultants are repackaging outdated thinking. In the age of digital technology, where you can customize your consumption, refine it, filter out unwanted noise, there is no such thing as the mass-media. Which is why the future belongs to those who understand what's at stake in the intimate conversation of the great record sleeve.

Primal Scream
Vanishing Point album
1997

Primal Scream
Vanishing Point album

1997

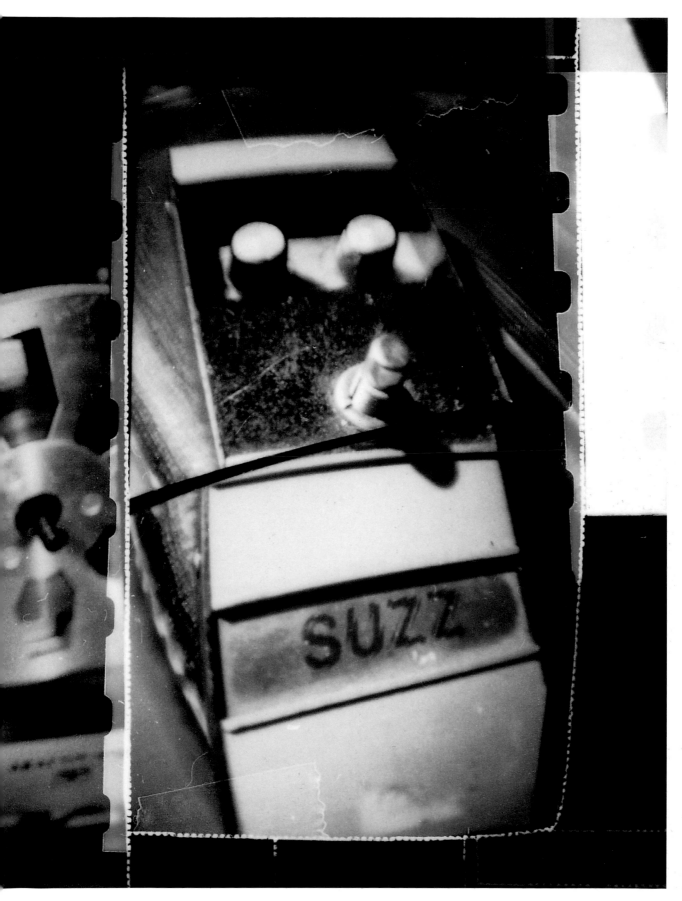

Primal Scream
Star single

1997

Date/Datum

Attention/zu Händen

Delivery Address/Lieferadresse

The Ragged School

Telephone/Telefonnummer	Facsimilie/Fax
T +44 [0] 20 7403 1316	F +44 [0] 20 7403 2954

S6

If licked induce vomiting and seek medical advice immediately.
Wenn Sie daran geleckt haben, Erbrechen herbeiführen und sofort einen
Arzt aufsuchen.

Ragged School location details Ragged School Adresse	E E
The Ragged School 47 Union Street London SE1 1SG	E them@theraggedschool.com www.theraggedschool.com

47

The Ragged School

Telephone/Telefonnummer

T +44 [0] 20 7403 1316

Facsimile/Fax

F +44 [0] 20 7403 2954

Date/Datum

S1 'Buyer' means the person who buys or agrees to buy the Goods from the seller.
'Der Käufer' ist die Person, die kauft oder einwilligt, die Waren vom Verkäufer
zu erwerben.

Ragged School location details
Ragged School Adresse

The Ragged School   E them@theraggedschool.com
47 Union Street
London SE1 1SG   www.theraggedschool.com

Q1 What is a reasonable excuse for not meeting the deadline?
Wie lautet eine vernünftige Entschuldigung dafür, einen Termin nicht einzuhalten?

For External Use

47 Union Street London SE1 1SG. VAT Number 548 00 80 54.

In a way it's a feast in a time of plague.

Es ist gewissermaßen ein Festmahl in den Zeiten der Pest.

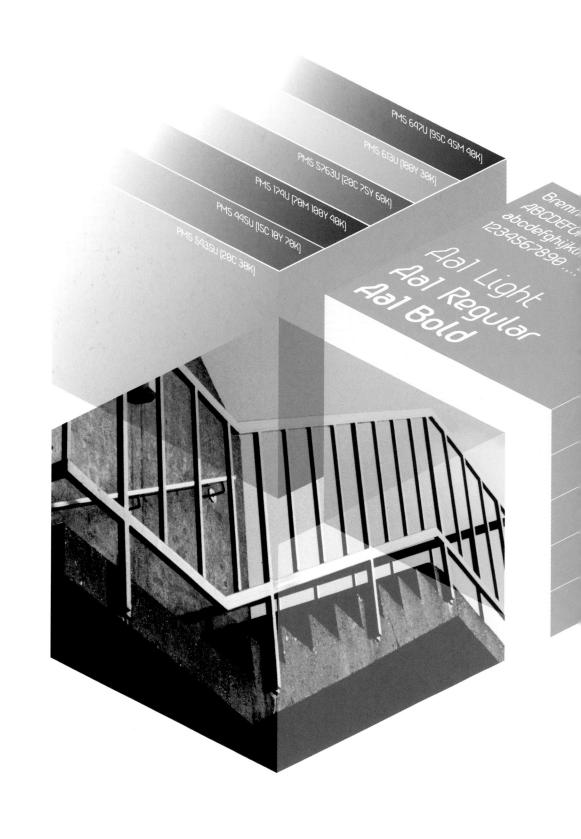

PMS 647U (95C 45M 40K)

PMS 613U (100Y 30K)

PMS 5763U (20C 75Y 60K)

PMS 174U (70M 100Y 40K)

PMS 445U (15C 10Y 70K)

PMS 5435U (20C 30K)

Bremi.
ABCDEFU
abcdefghijkl
1234567890 . . .

Aa1 Light
Aa1 Regular
Aa1 Bold

Mute
Identity

2000 >

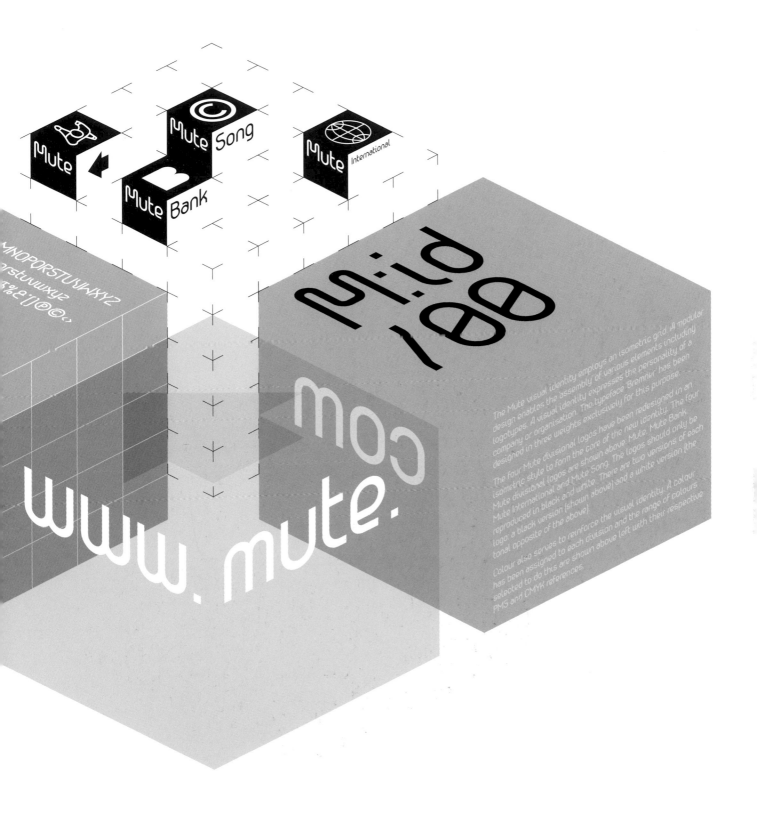

Mute

Mute Song

Mute Bank

Mute International

play

.com

www. mute.

The Mute visual identity employs an isometric grid. A modular design enables the assembly of various elements including logotypes. A visual identity expresses the personality of a company or organisation. The typeface 'Bremner' has been designed in three weights exclusively for this purpose.

The Four Mute divisional logos have been redesigned in an isometric style to form the core of the new identity. The four Mute divisional logos are shown above: Mute, Mute Bank, Mute International and Mute Song. The logos should only be reproduced in black and white. There are two versions of each logo: a black version (shown above) and a white version (the tonal opposite of the above).

Colour also serves to reinforce the visual identity. A colour has been assigned to each division and the range of colours selected to do this are shown above left with their respective PMS and CMYK references.

MNOPQRSTUVWXYZ
orstuvwxyz
%&?()@©,

Pantone 174
70M 100Y 40K

Pantone 613
100Y 30K

Pantone 5763
20C 75Y 60K

Pantone 647
95C 45M 40K

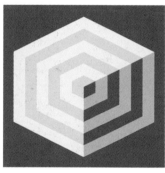

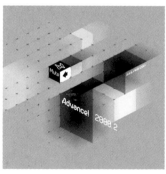

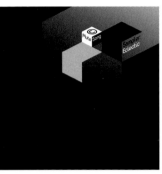

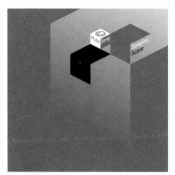

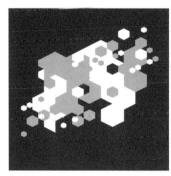

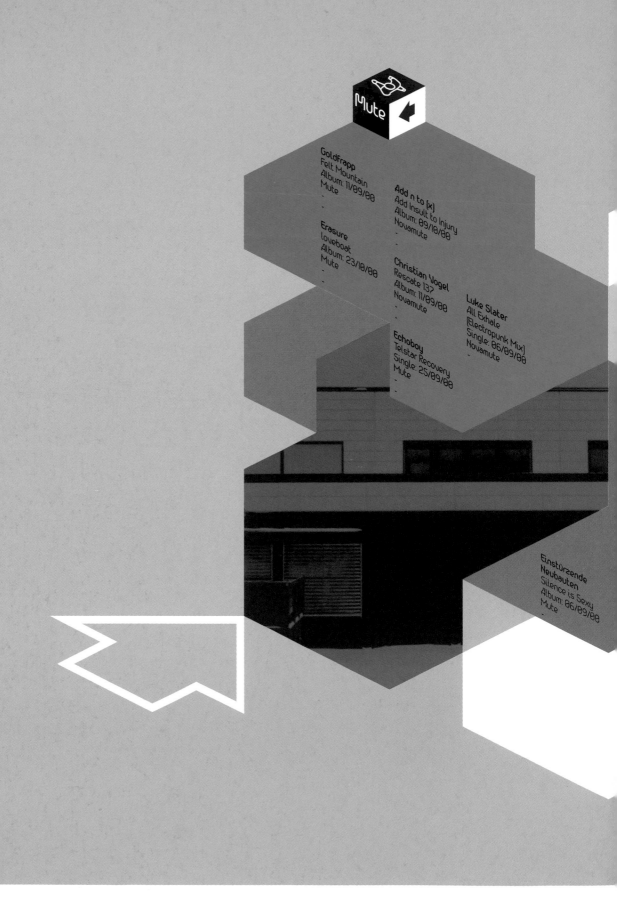

Mute

Goldfrapp
Felt Mountain
Album: 11/09/00
Mute
·

Erasure
loveboat
Album: 23/10/00
Mute
·

Add n to (x)
Add Insult to Injury
Album: 09/10/00
Novamute
·

Christian Vogel
Rescate 137
Album: 11/09/00
Novamute
·

Echoboy
Telstar Recovery
Single: 25/09/00
Mute
·

Luke Slater
All Exhale
(Electropunk Mix)
Single: 06/09/00
Novamute
·

Einstürzende
Neubauten
Silence is Sexy
Album: 06/09/00
Mute
·

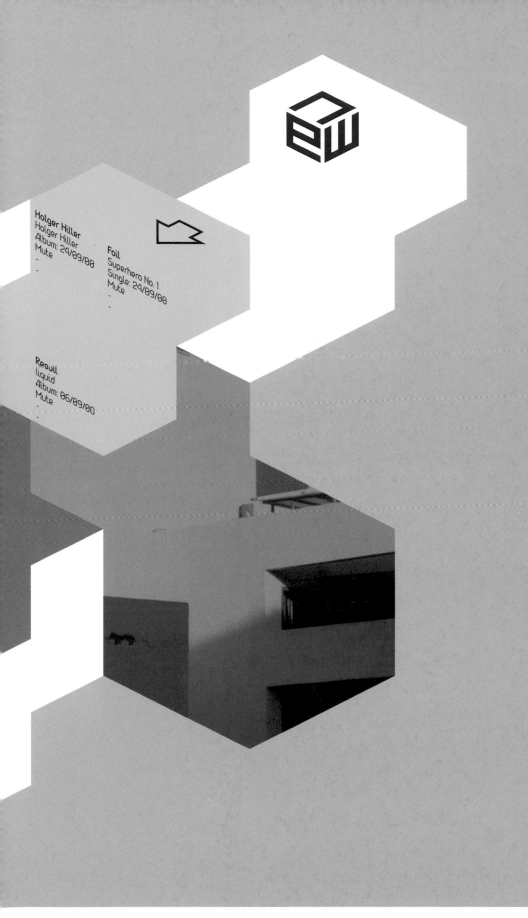

Holger Hiller
Holger Hiller
Album: 24/09/00
Mute
.
.

Foil
Superhero No. 1
Single: 24/09/00
Mute
.
.

Reoull
liquid
Album: 06/09/00
Mute
.
.

Malcolm McLaren
The Largest Movie House in Paris album

1995

 . Malcolm McLaren
The Largest Movie House in Paris album   . 1995

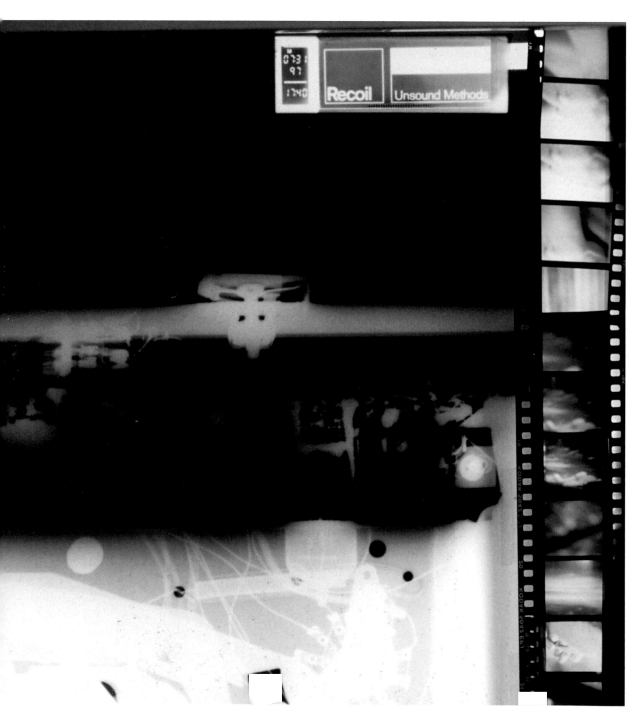

Recoil — Unsound Methods

Recoil
Unsound Methods album

1997

. Recoil
Unsound Methods album

. 1997

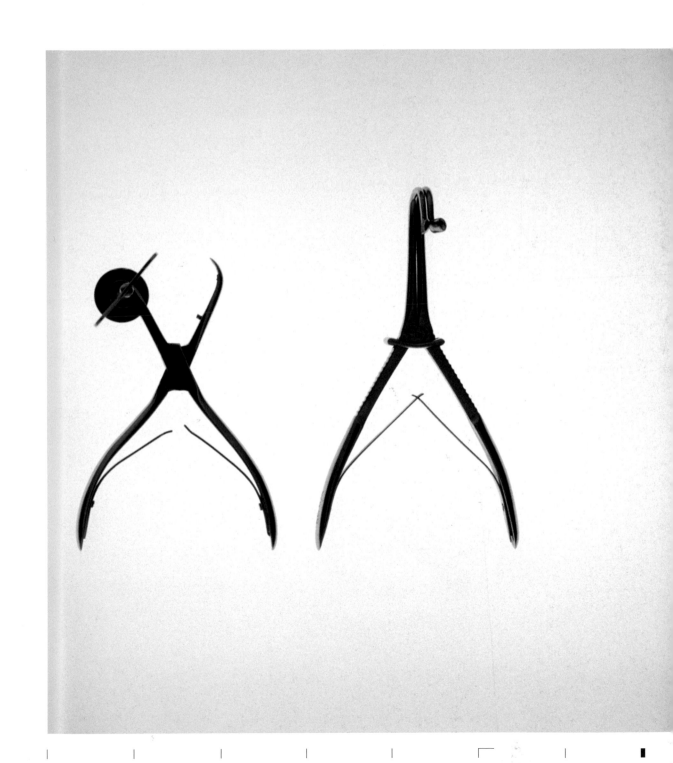

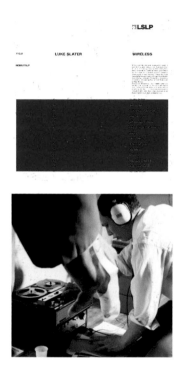

Luke Slater
Wireless album + singles

2000

◱LSEP

102.5   LUKE SLATER   ALL EXHALE#2

L12NOMU16

Postcards from the Edge | Itai Doron

Foreword

I received my first postcard back in the early seventies, when I was five or six. My father, who used to spend time away from home on business trips, asked my mother to join him in London, where he was staying at the time. He was missing her. I was left behind with my grandparents for a whole month. But it wasn't that bad, I loved staying with them.

One morning this illustrated postcard arrived – an English boy and a French girl 'reaching' over the English Channel to kiss. And I loved it. The message on the back was read to me and was nice too, but mostly it was the image.

Still my parents kept on sending more, and my grandmother suggested I should start a collection. I kept it in a little leopard-skin print box she gave me. I got hooked on wonderfully glossy pictures from exotic places.

The collection grew quickly. Whenever my parents, relatives or lucky schoolmates went abroad, they knew they had to send at least one postcard to add to my collection. Strangely, or so it seemed to me, I was never going places. I used to lie in bed with the box by my side, looking at the postcards endlessly, wondering what it was like in those faraway places. I wished I was there.

The next thing I got hooked on was the movies.

I guess I was fascinated with the blur between reality and fiction. I think in part it was to do with the fact that my grandmother used to take us to matinées every other day just to have some quiet time to herself. But it was also hearing my mother reminiscing about her adolescent rebel years, when she used to sneak out of school to a nearby cinema to watch Glenn Ford, Silvana Mangano, Natalie Wood, Warren Beatty and – above all – James Dean. These stories fuelled my imagination. I loved listening to her, humming the

theme song from Bitter Rice as she cooked pasta; talking about Deborah Kerr and Burt Lancaster every time she dipped her toes in the sea (to this day, she still can't swim); or telling me for the hundredth time how she fell for my father because he looked just like Al Pacino.

Movie moments were defining life itself. But when people asked me, mostly during my brief personal appearances at my parents' Friday night parties, 'What would you like to be when you grow up?' I used to say 'an artist'. This surprised my parents because I never created anything as a child. They expected to see something, but I was still searching for the right medium. And for a lengthy period of time during the nineties I thought I had found it – creating audio-visual installations.

This book is a record of those years. These photographs are not my 'art works', but mementoes from places I visited while preparing shows in local galleries. They were all shot with a fifteen-dollar camera I bought at Woolworths in LA.

These images mean more to me than just locations – going to Hollywood alone was a pilgrimage. As a child, these were the places I dreamed of visiting. Make-believe places that seemed to be on another planet.

I hope you will enjoy going there too.

Itai Doron, London, December 2000

Hollywood Memorial Cemetery, Los Angeles, CA, 1994

The Hollywood Sign, Mt. Lee, Los Angeles, CA, 1994

Los Angeles to Salinas, CA, 1994

I made a pilgrimage to Cholame (pop. 25), following the route that James Dean took the day he died. Dean was on his way to Salinas, where parts of East of Eden were shot, to attend a car race. He never reached his destination.

I wore light blue slacks, my white Jimmy T-shirt, and a pair of sunglasses. I started my journey ploughing through the early morning LA rush-hour traffic and arrived at Griffith Park where portions of Rebel Without a Cause were shot.

Back in the car and back to the freeway I headed toward Steinback country. I took the Ventura Freeway to Sepulveda Boulevard and then Interstate 5 through Bakersfield. From Wasco I took US 466 to the intersection with Highway 41, where I stepped out of the car.

Looking ahead I saw a naked stretch of highway that darted in and out of the California hills towards a giant sun. There were no other cars in sight and everywhere looked dry and lifeless it felt like a terrible place to die. I found a burnt California number plate on the side of the road and kept it as a souvenir.

I continued towards Cholame and pulled into Jack Ranch Cafe, a combination restaurant and gift shop. Inside I bought a coke and a copy of the Chronicle Tribune, dated 30th September 1955. Back in the parking lot I paused at a memorial to Dean outside the Cholame post office.

I carried on towards Salinas. I found the racetrack. The place was completely deserted and the temperature stifling. I visited the Firestone portable loo. Then I drove on to the track and for a few laps sped around like a racing driver. I was ready to take off.

Salinas, CA, 1994

UK   Germany   Europe   USA   Asia   Japan   Australia

Heather Dowling
Global Investment Banking
Baltimore

Christian Tellkamp
Global Equities
Frankfurt

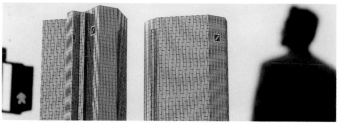

Your future with us	Leading to Results	Deutsche Bank	Global Investment Banking	Global Banking	Global Markets	Global Technology and Services
			Asset Management	Controlling and Finance		Global Equities

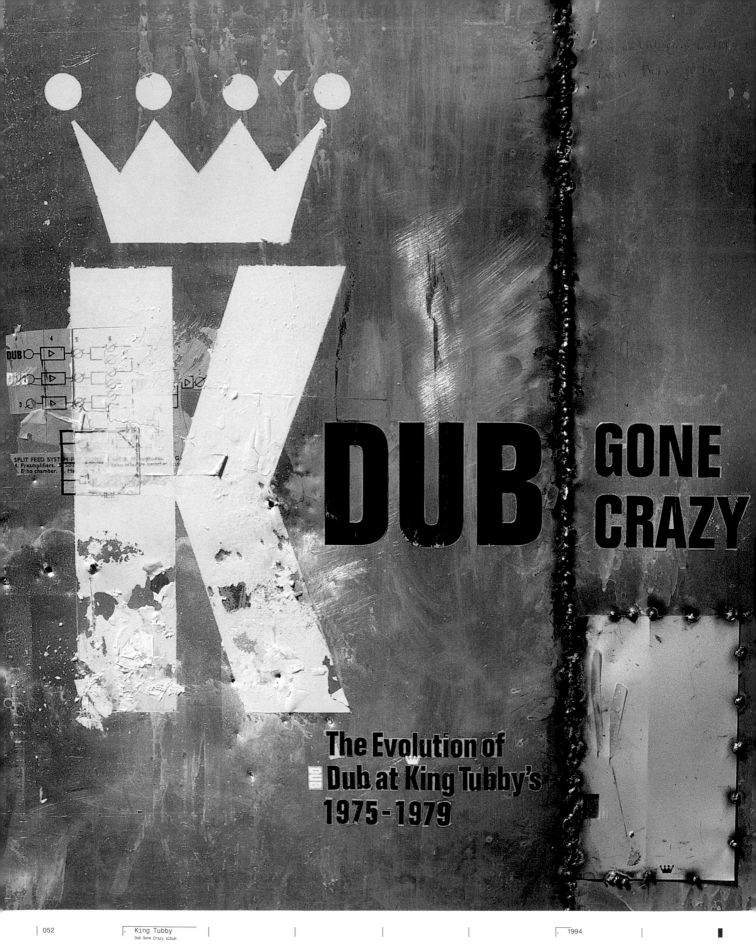

DUB GONE CRAZY

The Evolution of
Dub at King Tubby's
1975-1979

The Congos
Heart of the Congos album

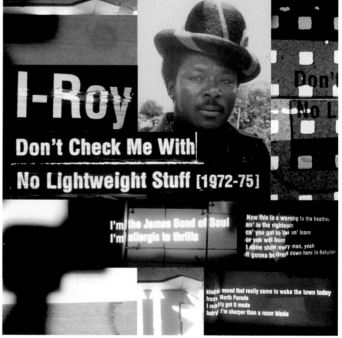

Blood and Fire

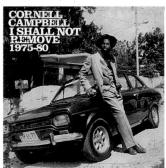

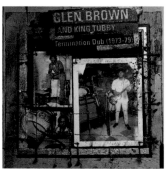

Yabby U
King Tubby's Prophesy of Dub album

1995

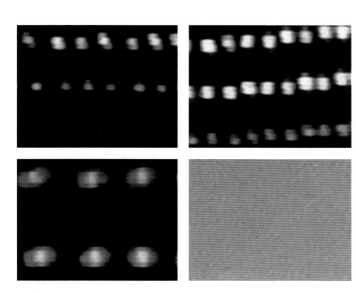

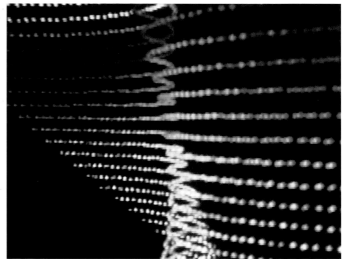

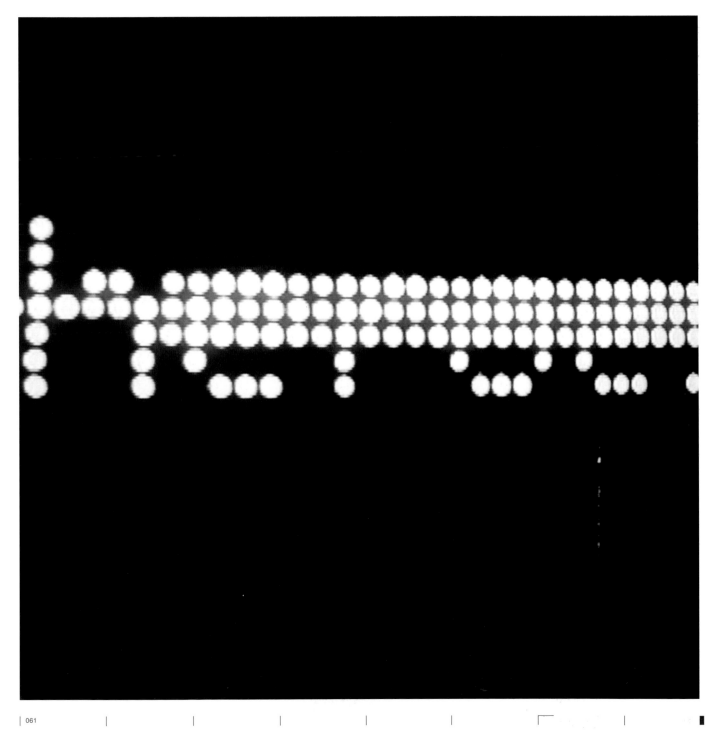

FOLK.

. Howie B
Folk album campaign posters

. 2001

FOLK.

HOWIE B FOLK.com

594 mm

500 mm

400 mm

300 mm

200 mm

100 mm

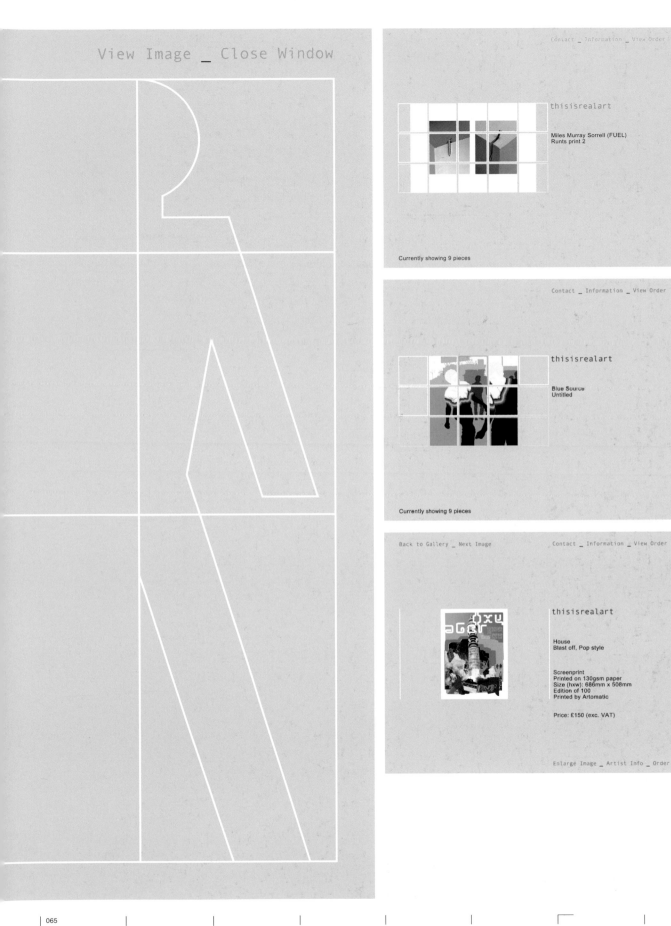

Contact _ Information _ View Order

thisisrealart

Miles Murray Sorrell (FUEL)
Runts print 2

Currently showing 9 pieces

Contact _ Information _ View Order

thisisrealart

Blue Source
Untitled

Currently showing 9 pieces

Back to Gallery _ Next Image

Contact _ Information _ View Order

thisisrealart

House
Blast off, Pop style

Screenprint
Printed on 130gsm paper
Size (hxw): 686mm x 508mm
Edition of 100
Printed by Artomatic

Price: £150 (exc. VAT)

Enlarge Image _ Artist Info _ Order

Thisisrealart
Numbered print

2001

PRML SCRM MTHR FCKR

Primal Scream
Exterminator album

PRML SCRM KILL ALL HIPPIES

one kill all hippies two sisterenator (massive attack remix)
three the revenge of the hammond connection, one written by
primal scream/unelson/discovery productions inc. (emi/copyright
control/complete music/copyright control/discovery productions
inc.) recorded by primal scream. produced by brendan lynch*
and primal scream. engineered by mac hayes. drums programmed
by keith tenniswood. the voice of linda eang is taken from the
film 'out of the blue' courtesy of discovery productions inc.
two written & recorded by primal scream (emi/copyright control/
complete music) produced by brendan lynch* and primal scream.
mix engineered by mac hayes. additional production and six by
del na/kevinshields, additional programming by alex swift. engineered
by les shepherd and dave jenkins. additional engineering by ben
findlay at real world. three written and recorded by primal
scream (emi/copyright control/complete music) produced by brendan
lynch* & primal scream engineered by mac hayes. vocals by lisa
eillet. trumpet by simon finch. *for lynchmob productions.
p&c 2000 creation records ltd. a creation records product. sleeve
by house@intro
dedicated to curtis mayfield

PRML SCRM SWSTK YS

one swastika eyes (chemical brothers mix) two swastika eyes
(pavlovs dog) three swastika eyes (edit) written and recorded
by primal scream.
track one: additional production by the chemical brothers.
engineered by steve dub, edited by steve dub and toby feltwell
additional production and mix by tom rowlands. track three:
additional production by the chemical brothers. engineered
by steve dub. edited by steve dub. radio edit in full & sides
for tunes bubbly music published by EMI/copyright control/complete
music (sleeve by house@intro) p & c 1999 creation records ltd
all rights re... the producer also the owner of the copyrighted...
this...

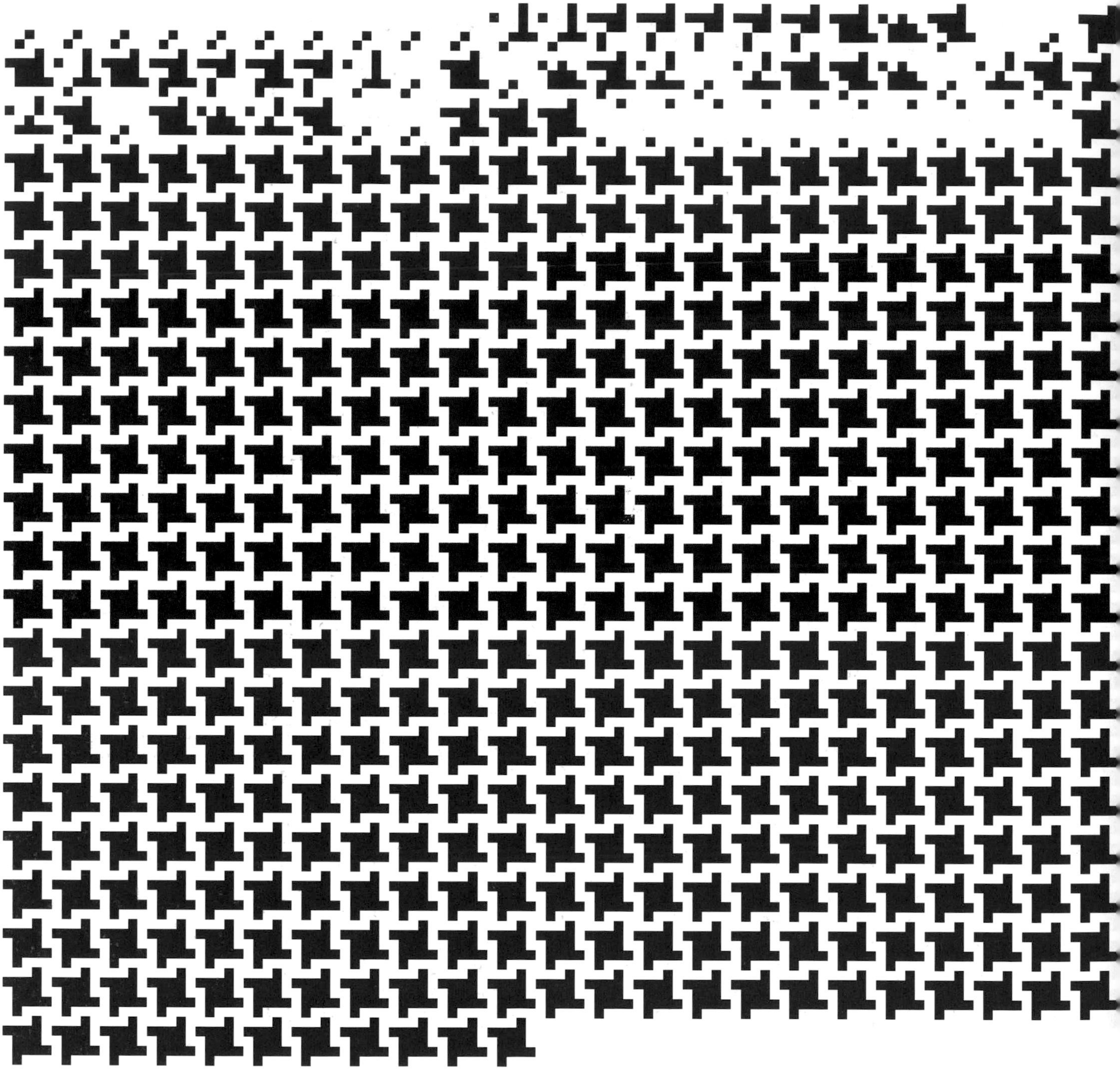

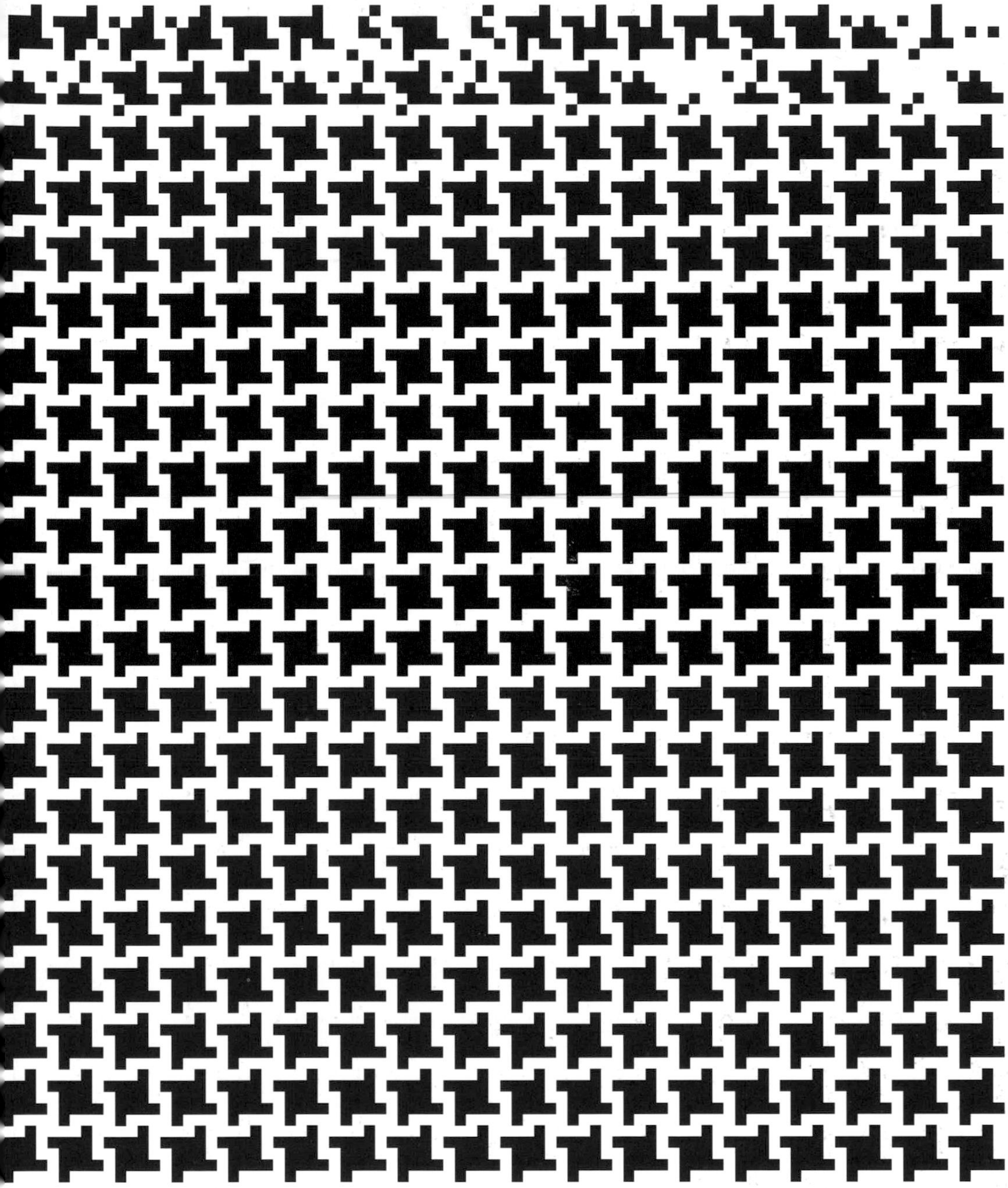

BIIIIIII   YOU CAN
FALL

IIII LP65

II IIIIII III IIII I II IRII D FOR
NO ONE YIIIIIIIIIIIIIIIIIIIIIII
TIII III IIIII IIIIIIIII II LATE IN
THE EVENING WHEN IT

BIIIIIIII   LOOK OUTI
                             SIDE

                        IIII LP65

IIIIIIII IIII IIII II IIII III   I IIII II IIII   IIIIIIII IIIIIII
IIII II IIIII IIII IIIIIIII IIII   IIIII IIIIIIII IIIIIIII IIIIIIII
III II IIII III IIIIII IIII IIII   II I IIII II II III
IIIIII IIII IIIII IIII IIIIIIII II   IIIIIIII IIIIIIII II
IIII IIIIIII IIII IIII IIIII IIII   IIIIIIII IIIIIIII IIII
III IIII IIIII II IIIII IIII II

IIII IIIIIIII AND WHEREVER I   IIIII IIIIII II I III III II
GO YOU ARE THERE YOU   IIIII IIIIIIII IIII II III II I
COLOUR IN THE   IIII III III II III IIII IIIII
EVERYDAI IIIIIIII I IIII II   IIIII IIII IIII IIIIIIII III
IIIII   IIIIIIII IIII IIIII IIIIIIII
IIIIIIII IIII IIII IIII IIIIIIII   IIIIIIII IIIIIIII IIIIIII
IIII IIIIIIII IIIIIIII IIIIIIII   IIII IIIIIIII IIIIIII II
III IIII IIIII IIII IIII IIII   IIIII III II III IIII II
II III IIIII IIII II IIII III   II III III IIII II IIII II

IIIIIIII IIII IIIIIIII IIIIIIII   IIIIIIII IIIIIIII IIIIIIII
IIIIIIII IIIIIIII IIIIIIII IIII   IIII IIIIIIII IIIIIIII IIII
IIIIIIII IIIIIIII IIII IIIIIIII   IIII IIIIIIII IIIIIIII III
IIIII IIII IIIIIIII IIII IIII   IIIII IIII IIIIIIII IIIII
IIIIIIII IIIIIIII IIII IIIIIIII   IIIIIIII IIII IIIIIIII
IIIIIIII IIIIIIII IIIIIIII IIII   IIIIIIII IIIIIIII IIII
IIII IIIIIIII IIII IIIIIIII IIII   IIII IIIIIIII IIIIIIII
IIIIIIII IIII IIIII IIII IIII II   IIIII IIII IIIIIIII III
IIII IIIII IIII IIIIII IIII IIIIIIII IIIII IIII IIII IIIIII

BIIIIIIII   COME ON
                             LET S GO

                             IIII LP65

RUN THE
UNTAIN SCARRED BY
VISIBLE BARS THE
ND WILL COME BLOW
SWER ECHOES ANSWER

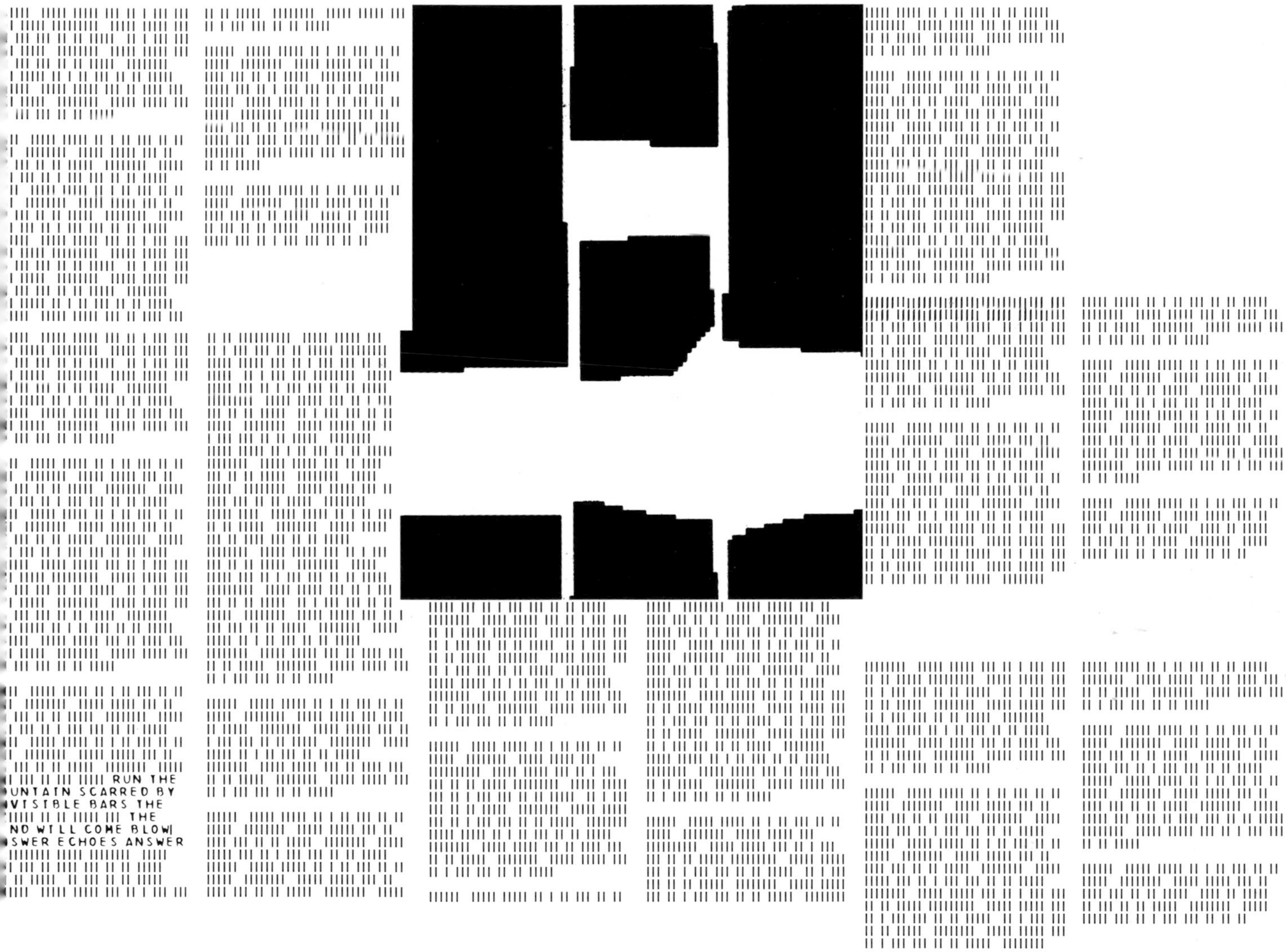

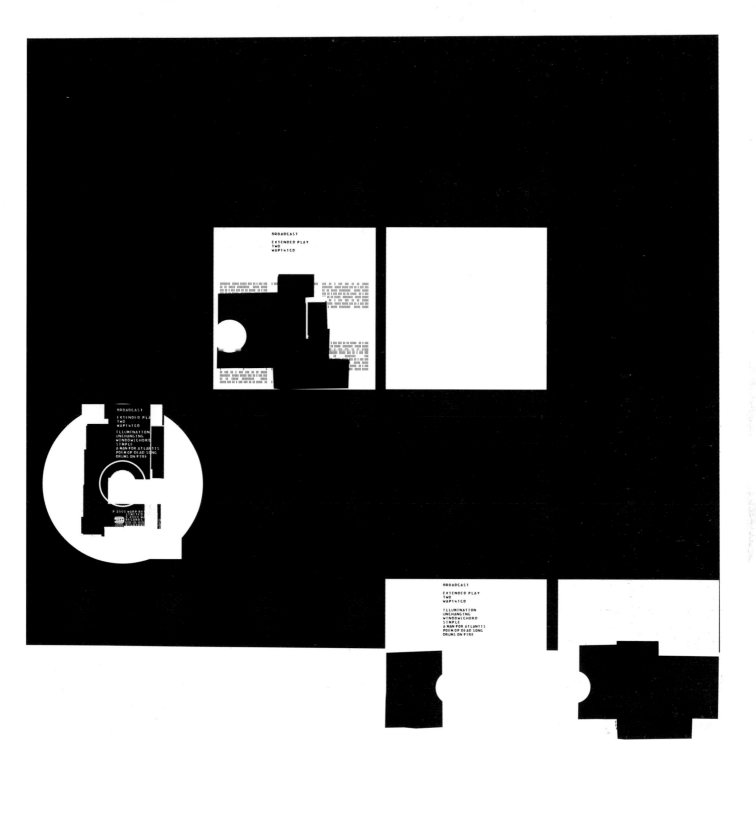

A1 Description of item (s)
Description des objets

A4 Description of item (s)
Ceci n'est pas un
nuage

A7 Description of item (s)
Description des objets
Cloud in the sky

A2 Intended use
Utilisation prévue des marchandises

A5 Intended use
Utilisation prévue des marchandises
Downer

A8 Intended use
Utilisation prévue des marchandises
:

A3 How do you feel today?
Cette copie appartient à?

>

A6 Description of goods
Description des objets

>>>>>>>>>>>>>>>>>>>>>>
>>>>>>>>>>>

A9 How do you feel today?
Cette copie appartient à?

>Like dancing

B1 Description of item (s)
Description des objets
Archive
Album> Take my head

B4 Description of item (s)
Description des objets

B7 Description of item (s)
Description des objets

C1 Description of item (s)
Description des objets

B2 Intended use
Utilisation prévue des marchandises
Upper

B5 Intended use
Utilisation prévue des marchandises

B8 Intended use
Utilisation prévue des marchandises
No use

C2 Intended use
Utilisation prévue des marchandises

B3 Fold along the dotted line
Plier suivant les pointillés

`

B6 Place and date of use
Lieu et date d'utilisation

>

B9 This copy belongs to
Cette copie appartient à

> > >

C3 Is this the end?
Est-ce la fin?

>yes

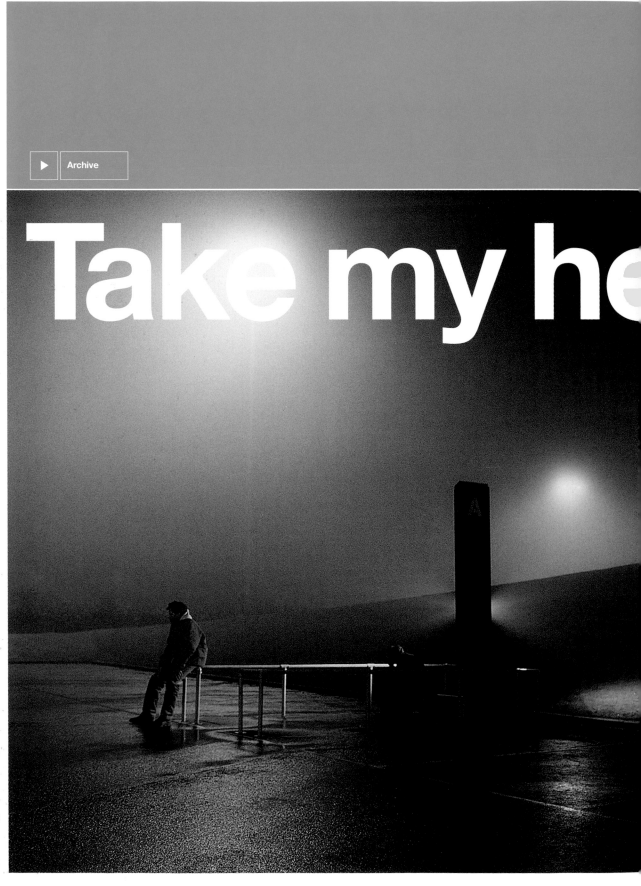

Take my he

A1 Description of item (s)

Archive album>
Take my head

ad

Q1 Is this the end?
Est-ce la fin?

Do not remove
Do not touch
Do not cover
Do not disturb
Do not ignore
www.archive-
web.com
Do not open until
Take my head

Mixed up

Do not remove

No loitering
No kissing
No loud music
No heavy petting
No overnight parking
No ball games
No naked flames
No removals
No entry
The way you love me

Single
Like dancing
Mixed up
A natural woman
Like surfing
www.archive-
web.com
Mighty real
You make me feel

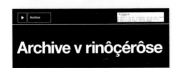

Archive v rinôçérôse

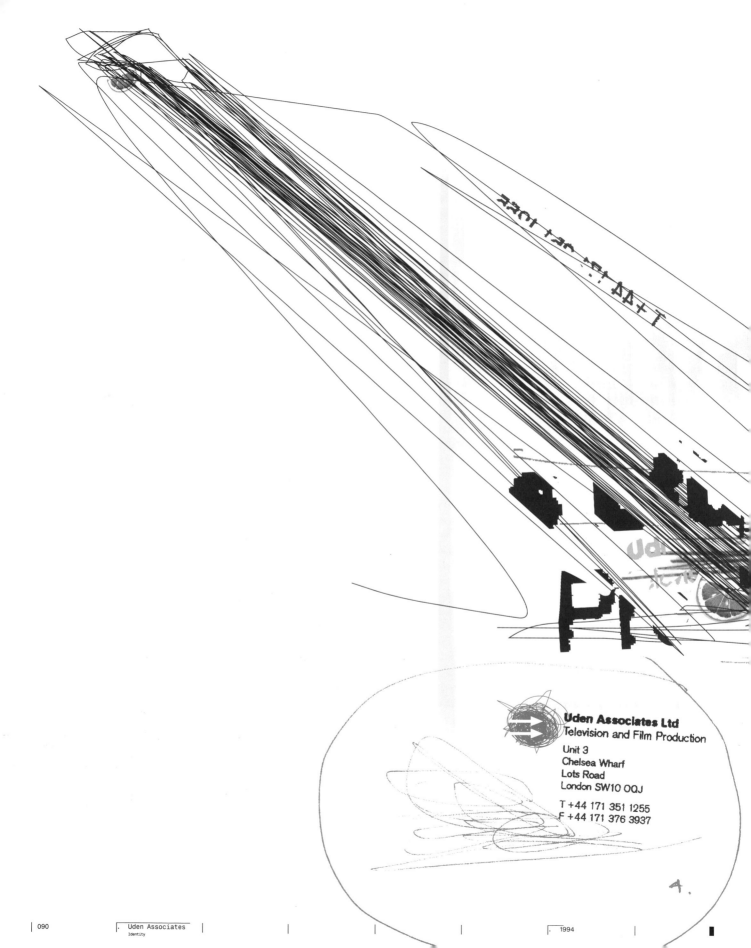

Uden Associates Ltd
Television and Film Production

Unit 3
Chelsea Wharf
Lots Road
London SW10 0QJ

T +44 171 351 1255
F +44 171 376 3937

4.

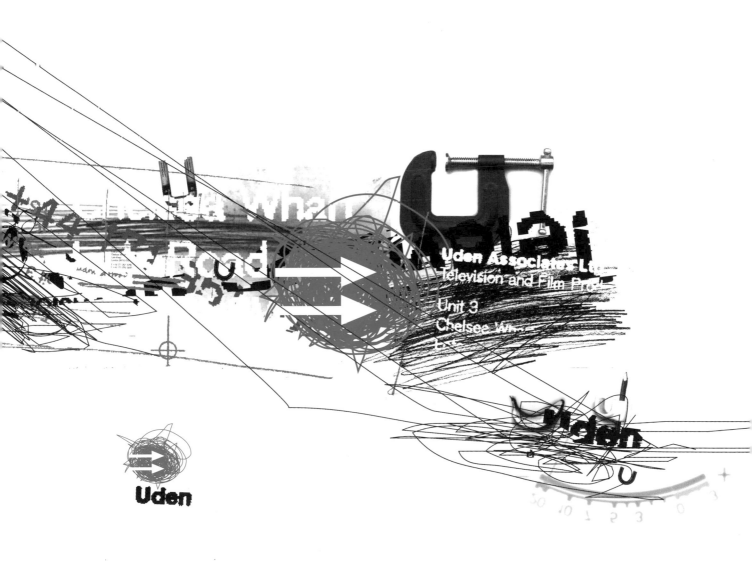

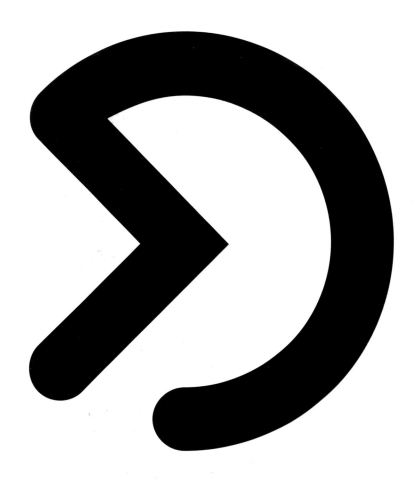

www.culturelab-uk.com
Website

2000

CULTURE LAB-UK

A users guide to style, culture and technology in the UK.

Massive Attack
A rare insight into the technology that drives the groundbreaking music of the Bristol-based band.

DESIGN
DIGITAL
FASHION-LAB
FILM
FUTURE
LIFE
MUSIC

UK GMT
23|01|01
12:40

View Flash site
Site requirements

The British Council

INFO-LAB
The Culture-Lab guide to education, industry and technology.

CULTURE LAB -UK

ARTICLES
DESIGN-LAB
DIGITAL
FASHION
FILM
FUTURE
LIFE
MUSIC

INFO-LAB
SEARCH GO

REGISTER

OPEN FORUM

The British Council

DESIGN-LAB

Design-Lab provides examples of the way science and technology are transforming the world around us.

1. LONDON EYE

In London, they've reinvented the wheel. Just to make sure you noticed, they made it 135 metres high. Then they plonked it right in the centre of the city.

Writer: Mark Irving

2. GREAT GLASSHOUSE

The Great Glasshouse in Wales is so environmentally sensitive that even the roof breathes.

Writer: Mark Irving

3. GOING UNDERGROUND

Unless you are the re-incarnation of a sardine, or a connoisseur of smells from Hell, travelling on London's underground was a test of your patience. But no longer.

Writer: Mark Irving

CULTURE LAB -UK

INFO-LAB
EDUCATION
INDUSTRY
LINKS

MAGAZINE
SEARCH

REGISTER

The British Council

INFO-LAB
The Culture Lab directory of who to watch, where to learn and the sites to visit

Welcome to Info-Lab!

Inside Info-Lab, the listings area of Culture Lab you'll find a whole load of useful information. There is a guide to the companies in the UK which are worth watching and are pushing the boundaries of technology, engineering and science in film, fashion, music, design, digital and life in general! The team at Culture Lab have also been out exploring the web to bring you information on a whole list of other interesting, exciting and useful sites for you to visit. And for those of you who have been excited by what you have read and what to see how you can get to know more and learn about science, engineering and technology, Info-Lab brings you a guide to relevant courses in the UK.

EDUCATION

Heading in the secondary font. Sub-head about fifteen to twenty words in length summarising the key features of this story.

INDUSTRY

Heading in the secondary font. Sub-head about fifteen to twenty words in length summarising the key features of this story.

LINKS

Heading in the secondary font. Sub-head about fifteen to twenty words in length summarising the key features of this story.

⌐. CultureLab
A3 poster
⌐. 2000

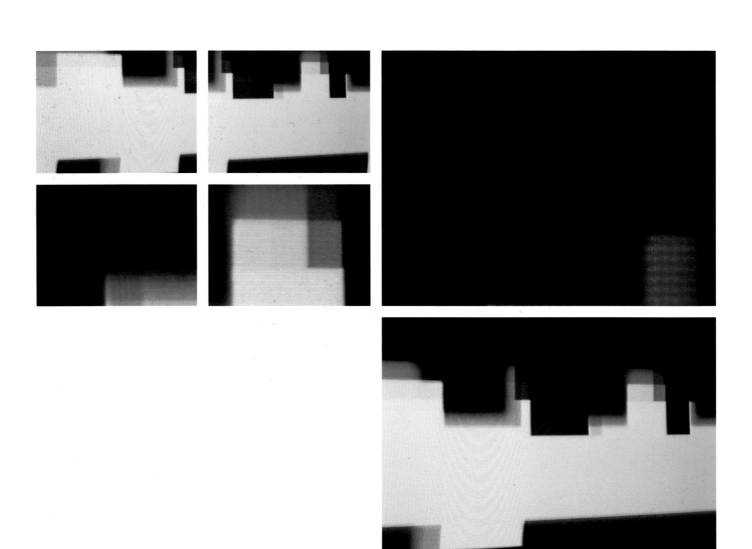

. Broad Band
A film

. 2000

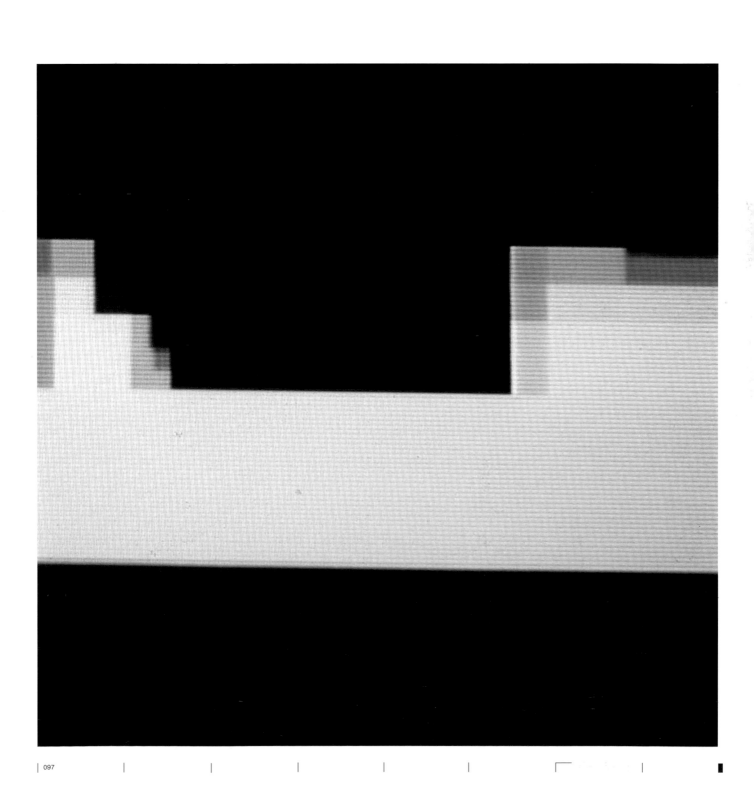

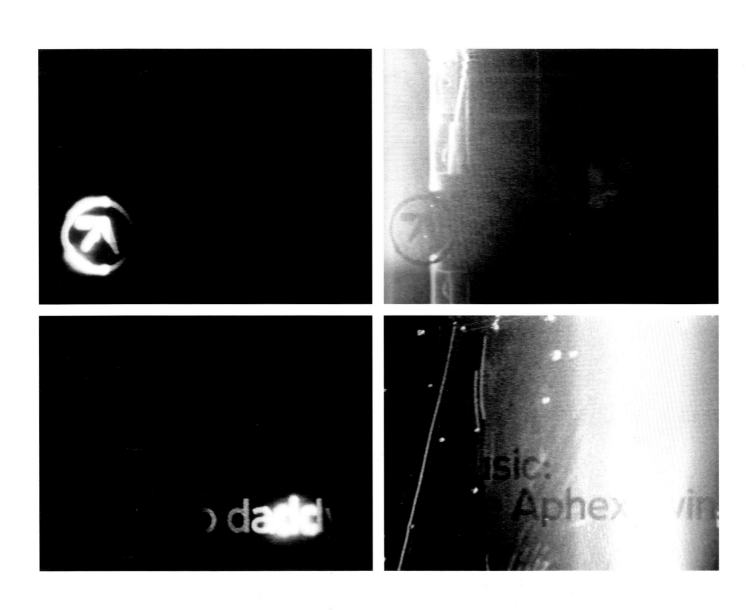

. Aphex Twin
Typography (Come to Daddy)
. 1997

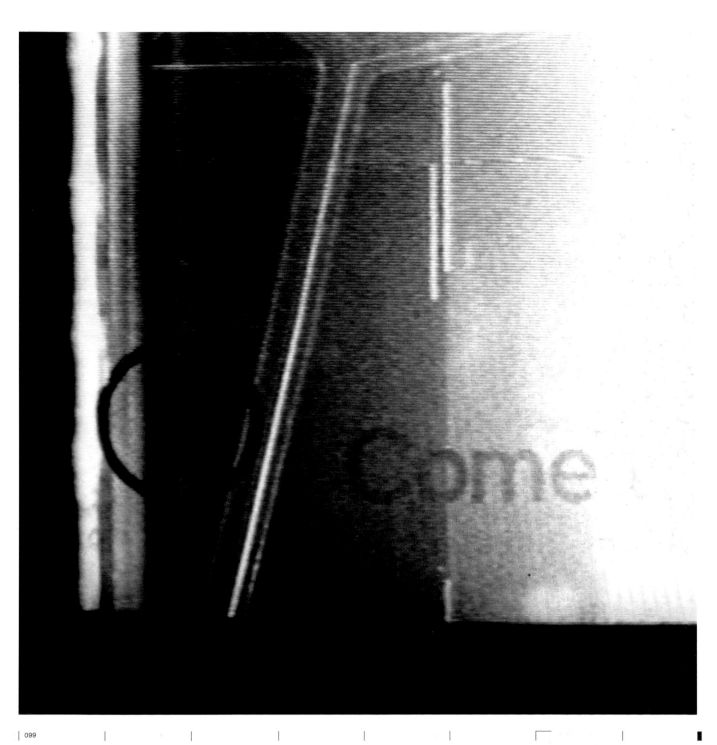

. INXS
Elegantly Wasted album
. 1997

INXS
Elegantly Wasted album

1997

Aged 18, Andy decided he wanted a change of scenery and packed his bags for London, where, within a year, he was playing music full-time. For several years, his free-wheelin' life was spent busking on the streets around the piazza in Covent Garden, jamming with musicians he met along the way and eventually landing a residency at Camden's grimy Dublin Castle playing acoustic blues sets. "I was learning my craft", says Andy, of his time touring the city he has made his home away from home ever since.

On returning to Glasgow for a year, Andy hooked up with Sace, who was looking for someone to voice two tracks he had demoed with Easi. Scraping up £100 between them, the trio went into the studio and recorded "Responsibilities" in one swift session. Easi and Sace played Andy the break they had selected and he wrote the song and lyrics on the spot. It's a track firmly rooted in the blues tradition and filtered through a hip hop sensibility. Over a jumpy string riff, Andy lays down an everyman philosophy of freedom. "If I can't have music, then there's nothing left," he wails, as if nailing down NT's reason for living in one clean take.

They intended to press up a thousand white label copies to garner some interest, but while DJing at a Stereo MCs after show party, Sace and Easi passed a tape of NT's tracks onto rapper Rob Hallam. The Stereo's manager was on the phone the next day raving about the tracks, beginning NT's long-standing relationship with the stalwarts of British hip hop. On the strength of hearing NT's tape, RCA gave the Stereo MC's, who were then riding high on success, their own subsidiary label called Natural Response. "Responsibilities" was released and the group set about recording an album.

In 1995, Sace and Easi started another club called Blueprint in the now-defunct Volcano club in the West End of Glasgow, where a lot of *Trainspotting*'s exteriors were filmed. A precursor to London's Scratch club, it featured Sace, Easi and guest DJs and bands playing a mix of soulful street music - hip hop, rare groove and reggae – in an environment that brought together breakdancers, graffiti artists and skateboarders (who made a ramp in one corner of the club). Hugely successful, the club often pulled in more punters on a Wednesday night than the venue drew on a weekend, and spawned its own fanzine, also put together by Easi and Sace. At the same time, NT were spending the rest of the week in the studio laying down tracks for their album.

But things didn't work out with RCA and both the label and NT were set loose from their obligations. With an album already in the bag the band remained without a deal for two frustrating years. That was until Nick Mander, the A&R at Epic who had signed Finley Quaye (who is himself signed to the Stereo MC's publishing company, Spirit Songs), heard the tape and after going to see NT rehearsing in Scotland, signed them. At this point they went back in the studio to freshen up the album and add a couple of new tracks with assistance from The Verve's engineer, Chris Potter.

In the intervening period, Sace and Andy have been honing their live show, which was given its first major airing on tour with Fun Lovin' Criminals at the close of last year. For those dates, they took on two new members, Richard and Mitch on percussion and bass respectively. They've also been recording new material which leans more towards live instrumentation which is sampled, looped and arranged. "We're more versatile now," says Andy, looking forward to the future. "You could call it regression. But it's in our bones."

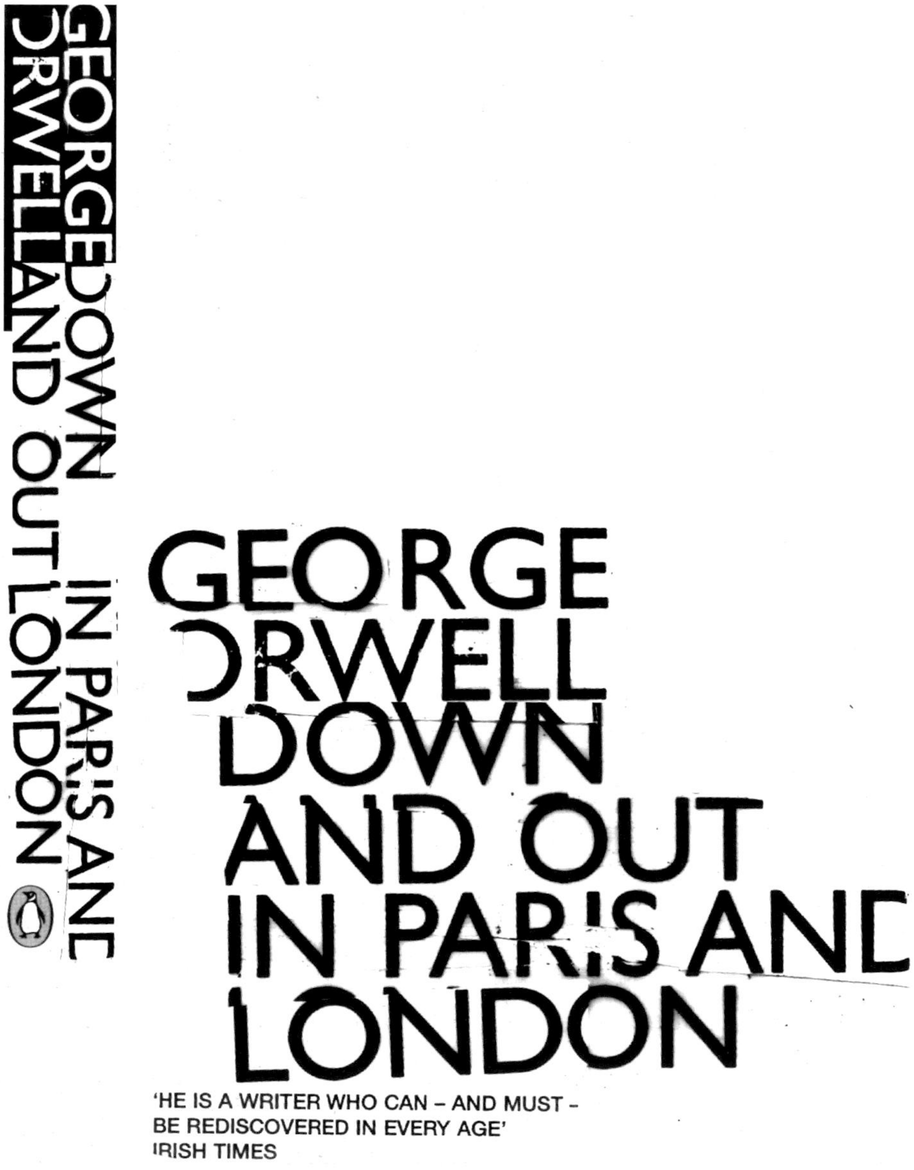

GEORGE ORWELL DOWN AND OUT IN PARIS AND LONDON

GEORGE
ORWELL
DOWN
AND OUT
IN PARIS AND
LONDON

'HE IS A WRITER WHO CAN – AND MUST –
BE REDISCOVERED IN EVERY AGE'
IRISH TIMES

Penguin
Book covers

1998 >

Kiss Me, Judas

Will Christopher Baer

Kiss Me, Judas

Will Christopher Baer

'Marvellous... If there was a Booker just for opening chapters, this would be in with a shot' *Maxim*

Goodbye to AllThat
Robert Graves

'His wonderful autobiography'
Jeremy Paxman, Daily Mail

Goodbye to AllThat
Robert Graves

HUNTER S. THOMPSON
HELL'S ANGELS

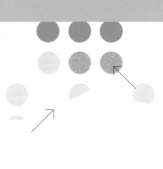

R.C. LEWONTIN

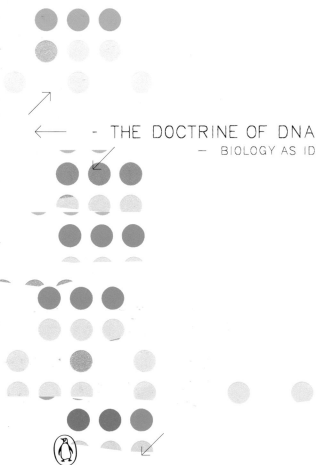

R.C. LEWONTIN – THE DOCTRINE OF DNA

← – THE DOCTRINE OF DNA
– BIOLOGY AS IDEOLOGY

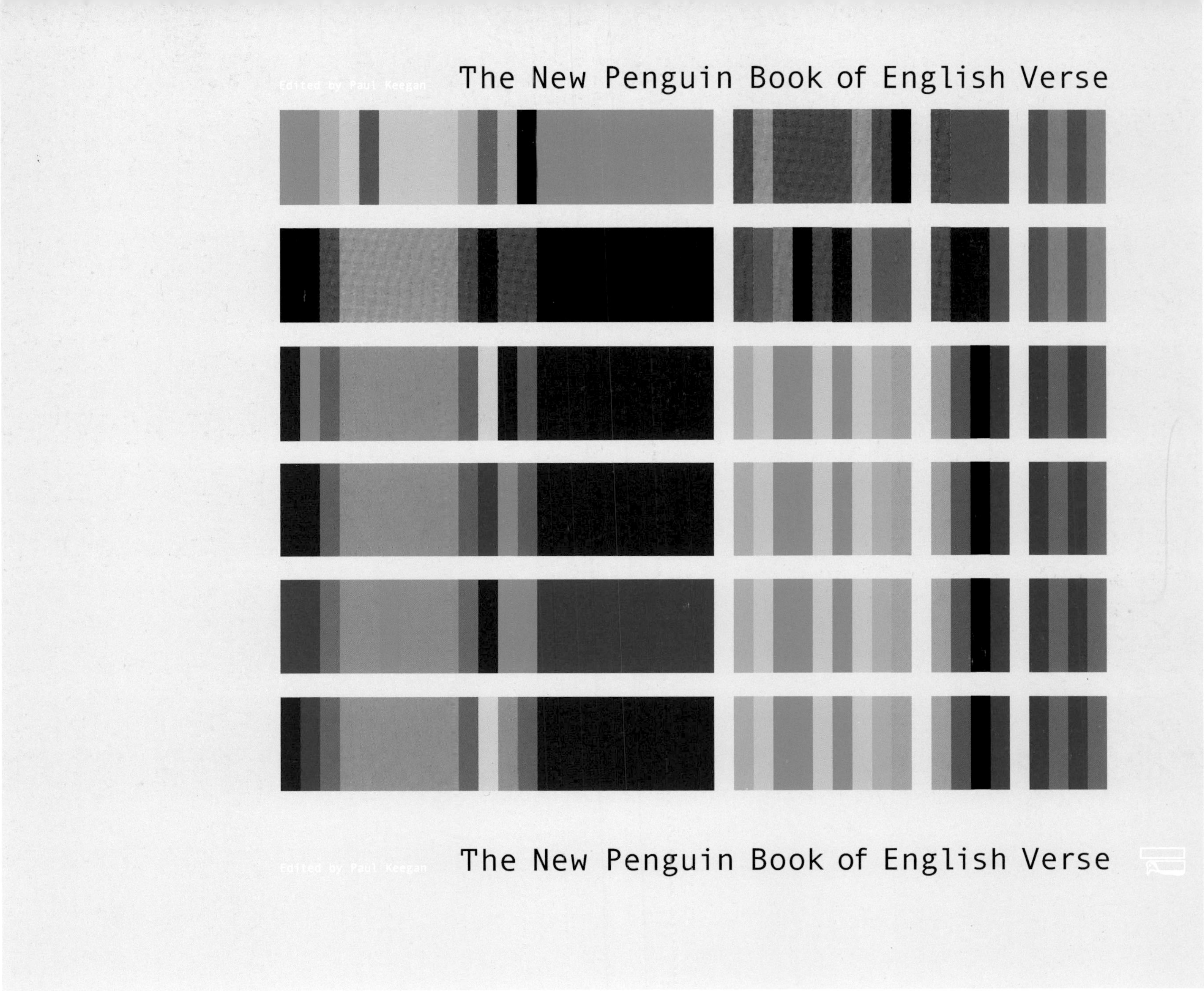

Edited by Paul Keegan

Edited by Paul Keegan

The New Penguin Book of English Verse

The New Penguin Book of English Verse

Barry Adamson As above So below

Barry Adamson
As Above So Below album

1998

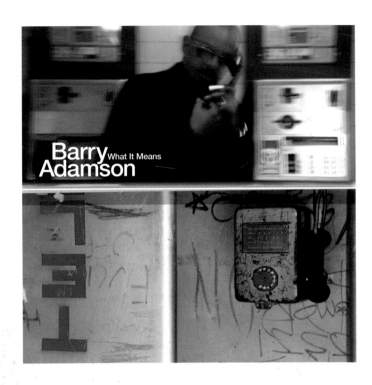

Barry Adamson**Can't Get Loose**

. Fusion
Logo design

. 1999

usht.ion

X

[G.M]
gimme
music.co.uk

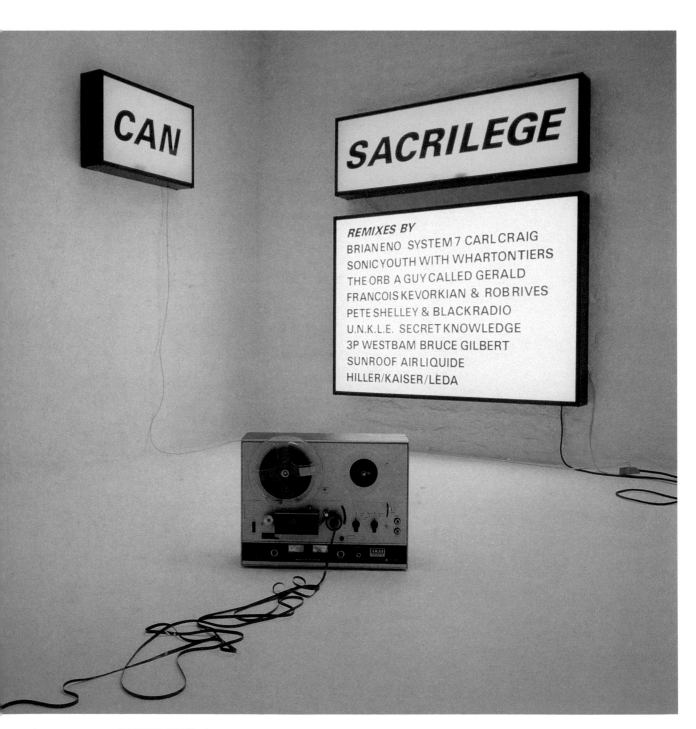

Can
Sacrilege album and book cover

1997

. The Nicoteens
Planet X album cover art
. 1998

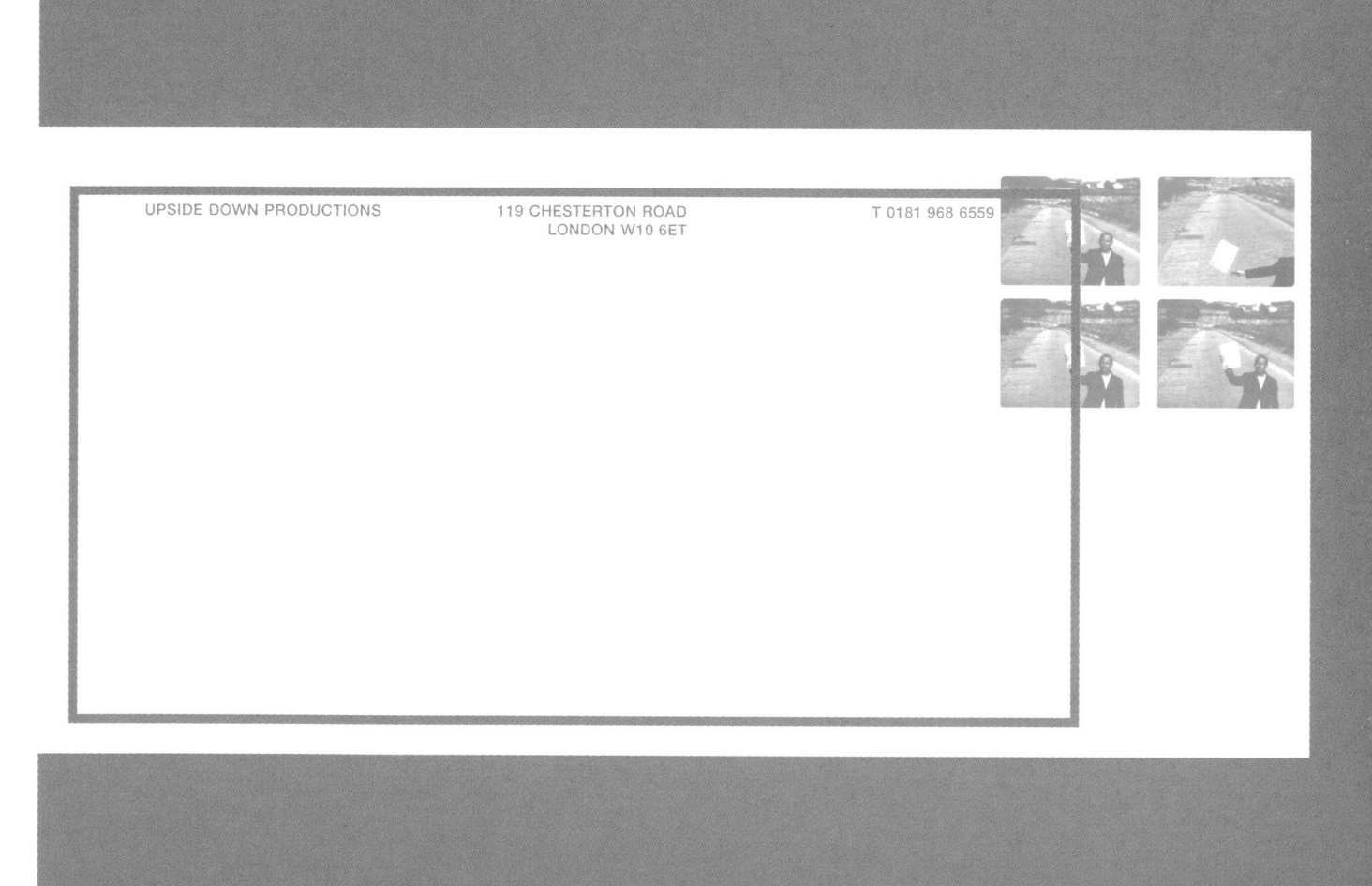

UPSIDE DOWN PRODUCTIONS   119 CHESTERTON ROAD   T 0181 968 6559
LONDON W10 6ET

UPSIDE DOWN PRODUCTIONS

119 CHESTERTON ROAD
LONDON W10 6ET

T 0181 968 6559

Rogue Films
–   –
–   –

177 Wardour Street   Telephone   E-mail: A Rogue Trader
Soho London   44 [0]171 434 2222   mail@roguefilms.co.uk
W1V 3FB   Facsimile   –
–   44 [0]171 494 7808

Primal Scream
Kill All Hippies video

2000

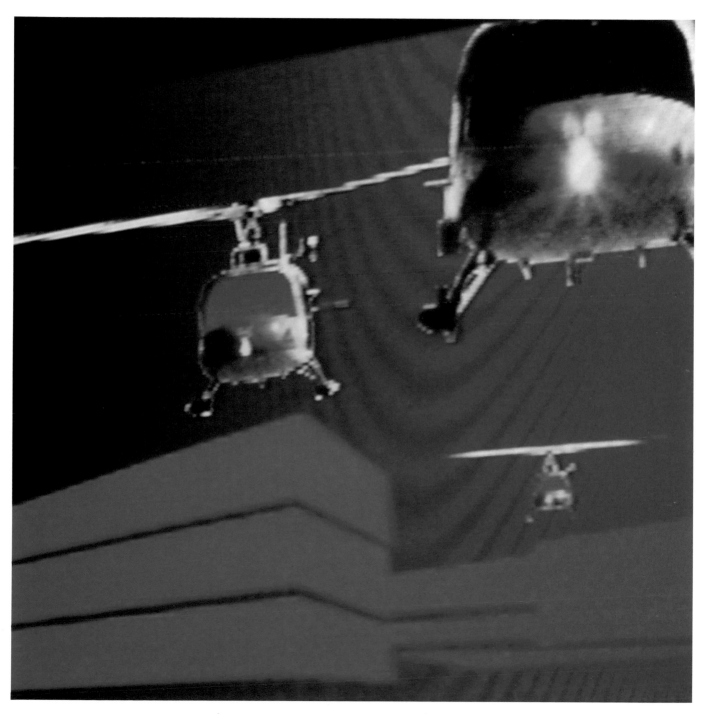

FEEDER

Feeder
Yesterday Went Too Soon album

. Feeder
Yesterday Went Too Soon album
. 1999

Side 1	Traveller
	Butterfly
Side 2	Cutrix
	Mombasstic
	Decca
	Eclipse
Side 3	OK
	Light
	Disser/Point.Mento.B
Side 4	Soni
	Vikram the Vampire

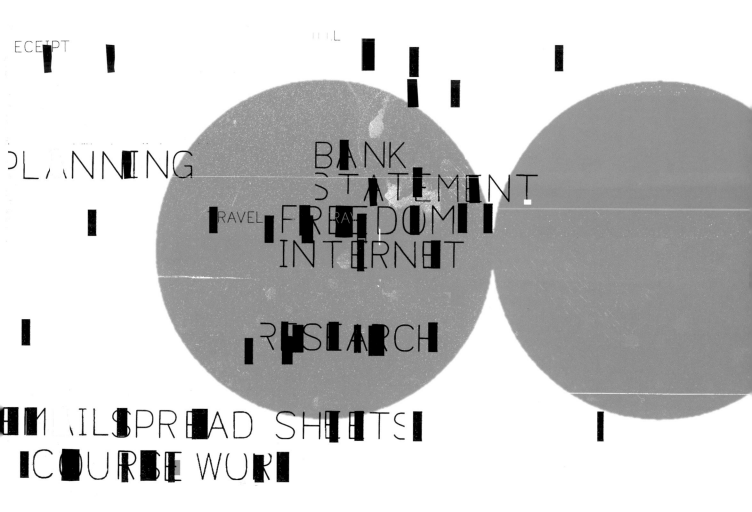

RECEIPT

PLANNING

BANK
STATEMENT
TRAVEL FREEDOM
INTERNET

RESEARCH

EMAIL SPREAD SHEETS
COURSE WORK

140   Key Skills   2001
Government education initiative

3

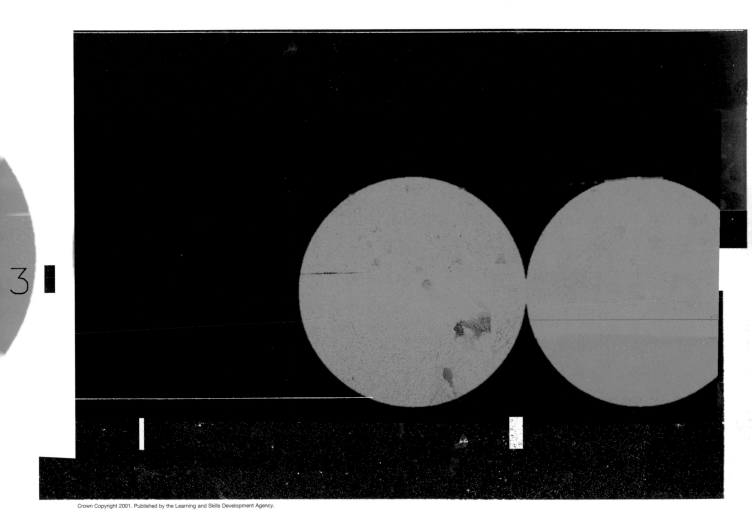

20
Dance Records
That Shook
The World

This is in no way meant to be a definitive list. Neither is it meant to be the best records ever made. It is, however, a modest list of records that we believe shaped the way that dance music is today.

Some of these records are nearly thirty years old; some were made in the nineties. Some don't sound so great today; some are still fantastic and still get played.

If you owned these twenty, you would know how dance music came to sound like it does today.

Visiting the can be an

The DJs

ouble nce.

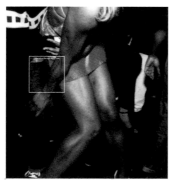

suits are

Nightlife's
Day Job

are ey g

a dangero

Visiting the Ministry of Sound in the daytime can be an unusual experience. Today looks like trouble: there's a police car blocking the entrance. Hordes of middle-aged people in suits are pouring out of the club and the cops are eyeing them as if these businessfolk were...

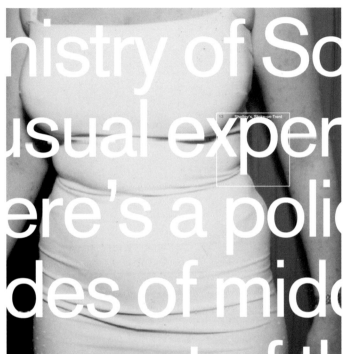

nistry of Sound in the c
usual experience. Toda
ere's a police car bloc
des of middle-aged pe
ng ot e clu
m as se bus
gang c ligans

The Culture

The Bands

It doesn't take a Ph.D to make you realise that music and dancing go hand-in-hand. Motown was dance music, everyone knows of James Brown and George Clinton's contributions and even rock acts often managed to slip an uptempo number on their albums. Bands have always been central to dance: here are six which made more of a difference than most. Respect also to The Chemical Brothers, Stone Roses, Underworld, Leftfield, Orbital, Massive Attack, Stereo MCs, New Order.

13   Shelley's, Stoke-on-Trent

The History
of DJing and
the 'Origins
of House

The Godfather o
known Brooklyn-
Grasso. Althougl
immediate post-v
discotheques firs
and London in the
the **Sanctuary** tha
blueprit for what
DJs had aithar ta

he modern DJ is a little

orn man called Francis

DJs had emerged in the

ar period, with prototype

opening in Paris, New Yo

sixties, it was at a club ca

Grasso laid down the

as to follow. Previously,

3: Business Card

2: Compliment Slip

1: Letterhead

Modalit Ltd
56 Cavendish Rd, London, SW19 2EU
T: 020 8542 7899
F: 020 8542 7887
enquiries@modalit.com
www.modalit.com

Modalit

NOTHING ELSE   ARKCD 004
E 327 558   20.15
N 642 918   23.05.96

NOTHING ELSE ARKCD 004
20.15
E327 558
N642 918
23.05.96

ARCHIVE

SO FEW WORDS   ARKCD 002
E530 040   20.48
N180 370   02.05.96

So Few Words single

LONDINIUM
E551 858
N097 478

ARKCD 002
15.34
06.05.96

Lou Harrison
Piano Concerto

Joanna MacGregor

sound
circus

SoundCircus
A2 poster

1998 >

SoundCircus
New sounds for open ears
| | | | | | | | | | |
www.soundcircus.com

Design and photography by Intro

SoundCircus
CD packaging

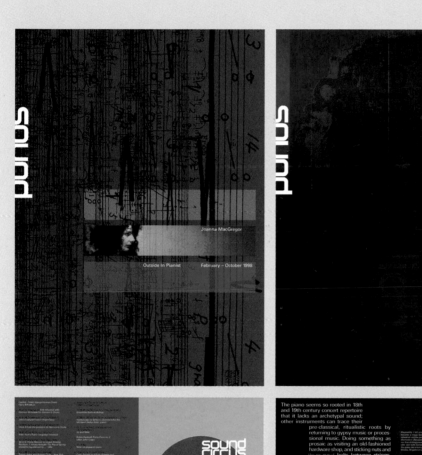

sound

Joanna MacGregor

Outside In Pianist   February – October 1998

sound

sound
circus

The piano seems so rooted in 18th
and 19th century concert repertoire
that it lacks an archetypal sound;
other instruments can trace their
pre-classical, ritualistic roots by
returning to gypsy music or proces-
sional music. Doing something as
prosaic as visiting an old-fashioned
hardware shop, and sticking nuts and
bolts between strings,
seems to transport the
piano back through time.

sound
circus

STEREOLAB MISS MODULAR

1 Miss Modular 2 Allures

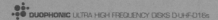 **DUOPHONIC** ULTRA HIGH FREQUENCY DISKS D-UHF-D16s

. Stereolab
Dots and Loops album

. 1997

stereolab dots and loops

1 Brakhage 2 Miss Modular 3 The Flower Called Nowhere 4 Diagonals 5 Prisoner of Mars 6 Rainbo Conversation 7 Refractions in the Plastic Pulse 8 Parsec 9 Ticker-tape of the Unconscious 10 Contronatura

 DUOPHONIC ULTRA HIGH FREQUENCY DISKS D-UHF-CD17

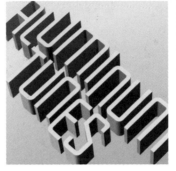

COBRA AND PHASES GROUP PLAY VOLTAGE
IN THE MILKY NIGHT

STEREOLAB

Depeche Mode
The Singles 86-98 album

1998

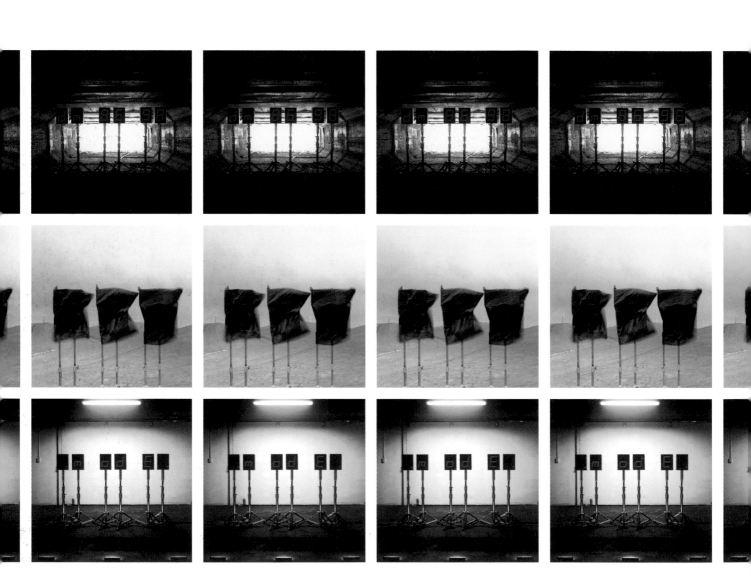

Depeche Mode
The Singles 86-98 album

1998

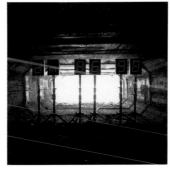

Depeche Mode
Only When I Lose Myself single

1998

Factory Too
A Factory Sample Too 7" gatefold

1995

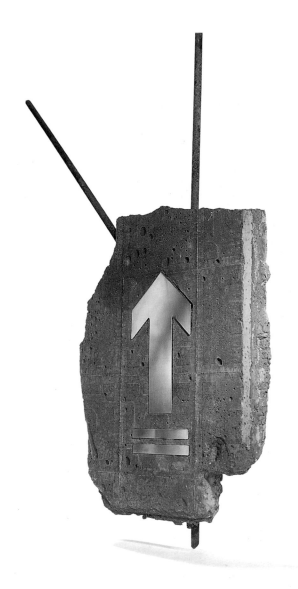

FACD2.02 A Factory Sample Too

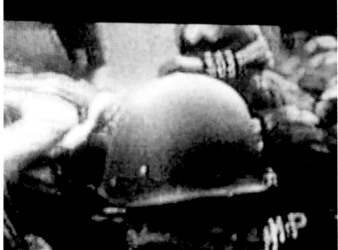

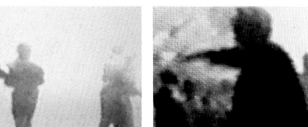

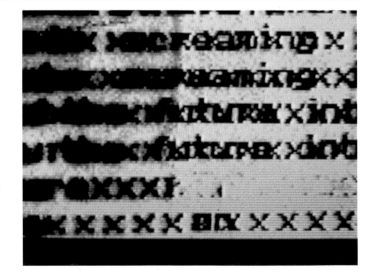

Primal Scream
Accelerator video

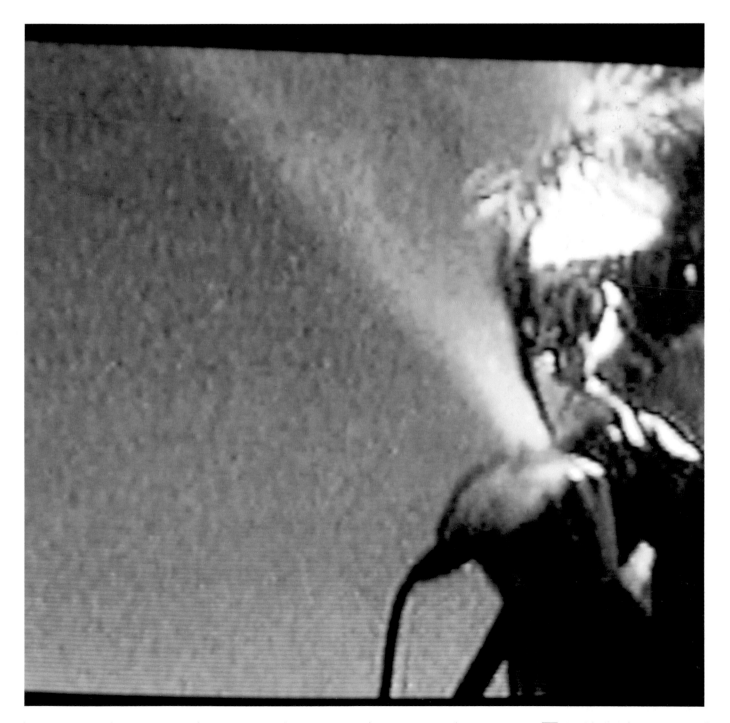

Grands Land
TV promo

. 2001

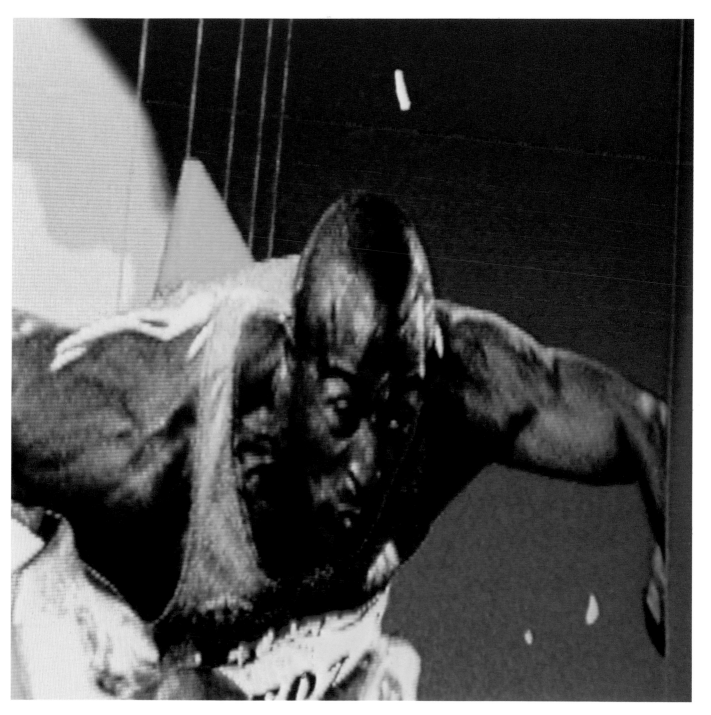

Blue Spring Capital
Identity
2001

Blue Spring Capital

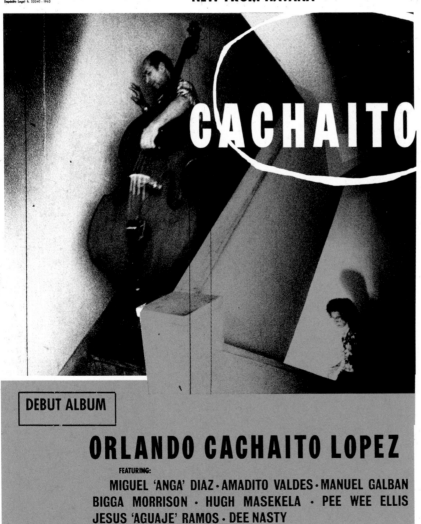

Orlando Cachaito Lopez
Cachaito poster + album   2001

. Robbie Williams .   . 1996
Life Thru a Lens album

Robbie Williams
Life Thru a Lens album

Page	Client	Project	Credits	Details
018	Creation	**Primal Scream** **Vanishing Point**	Design and art direction: Intro Original photography: Paul Kelly	Spreads from gatefold Primal Scream album cover. Speed kills on the Westway; homage to Barry Newman in a red Dodge Challenger.
022	Creation	**Primal Scream** **Star**	Design: Intro Photography: Ron Riesterer	Front and back cover from 12" sleeve showing Black Panther Bobby Hutton. Photograph taken by *Oakland Tribune* photographer Ron Riesterer June 1967. Single released June 1997.
024	Zanna	**The Ragged School** **Identity**	Design: Intro	Identity and stationery for fashion photographer Zanna.
028	Mute	**Mute** **Identity**	Design: Intro Photography: Angela Hayward [page 028] Simon Svard [page 032]	Various extrapolations of Mute Records visual identity. We received two stipulations from Mute boss Daniel Miller: retain the Mute man and never refer to the project as 'corporate identity'.
034	No!	**Malcolm McLaren** **The Largest Movie House in Paris**	Design and art direction: Intro Photography: Zanna	Cover art for Malcolm McLaren ambient album. The block of ice took four days to melt, with the help of a pneumatic drill.
038	Mute	**Recoil** **Unsound Methods**	Design and art direction: Intro Photography: Merton Gauster	X-rays and surgical implements. Recoil is musical vehicle for Alan Wilder, former keyboard player with Depeche Mode.
042	Mute	**Luke Slater** **Wireless**	Design and art direction: Intro Photography: Nigel Bennett	Mute techno artist in surveillance mode. Reference: Francis Ford Coppola's *The Conversation* and pulp fiction book jackets.
044	Itai Doron	**Itai Doron** **Postcards from the Edge**	Book design: Intro Original photography: Itai Doron	*Postcards from the Edge*. Photographs by artist and cinephile Itai Doron, showing his obsession with Hollywood and other aspects of popular culture.
048	Deutsche Bank	**Graduate recruitment campaign**	Design and art direction: Intro Photography: Andy Earl Styling: James Sleaford	Global campaign for Deutsche Bank's annual graduate recruitment programme. Shot in Singapore, England, USA, Japan and Germany.
052	Blood and Fire	**Blood and Fire** **Cover art**	Design and art direction: Intro	Series of installations, sculptures and dub art for leading reissue label Blood and Fire. Check out the chat room on www.blood andfire.co.uk for comments [pro and con] on the Blood and Fire artwork.
060	Talkin' Loud	**Roni Size** **Heroes**	Film direction and production: Intro	Multi-layered music video combining live action and digital graphics for single by Bristol-based beat scientist Roni Size.
062	Polydor	**Howie B** **Folk**	Design and art direction: Intro Photography: Toby Glanville	Mummers celebrate new Howie B album: Wicker Man meets techno-pagan folk ritual in English countryside. www.howiebfolk.com

Display Copy Only

Dedicated to: Steve Barrow – selector, dub master and friend.

Special thanks to: Philip de Nahlik for wise counsel and tolerance beyond the call of duty; Nena Antiporda for looking after us; Barry Boston our benign landlord; Paul 'I'm not an estate agent' Kemsley; all the splendid people who've worked at Intro over the past decade; and finally our wonderful and far-sighted clients, without whom…

Heartfelt thanks to all those involved in the work featured in this book: Barry Adamson, Matt and Yve Akehurst, Lloyd Anderson, Ray Anker, Mark Anthony, Roya Arab, Doug Armstrong, Peter Arnold, Sally Ann Arthur, Laurence Aston, Mark Austin, Howie B, Lu-lu Baring, Tom Betterton, Andy Blake, Steve Blonde, Lord Brocklehurst, Roland Brown, Peter Browne, Cindy Burnay, Marie Burmiston, Sgt. Mick Byard of Holborn Police, Cally Calloman, Nadia Capy-Osgood, James Cargill, John Chuter, Tim Clarke, Monica Clements, Lee Collins, Ben Cook, John Copper, Jo Cosbert, Paul Craig, Tony Crean, Charlie Crompton, Chris Cunningham, Paul Cushion, Holger Czukay, Davo, Andy Dodd, Charlie Dombrow, Itai Doron, Nicole Doukas, John Downe, Vivienne Dykstra, Edmundo, David Eindhoven, Yasmine El Ghamrawy, Miko Eley, Vanessa 'Scuze' Elliot, Richard Engler, Peter Evans, Liz Faber, Andrew Farris, John Farris, Tim Farris, Tim Felton, John Ferguson, Andrew Fletcher, Chris Francis, Insp. Graham French of Holborn Police, Dave Gahan, Kat Galer, Tim Gane, Gary Garry Beers, Bobby Gillespie, Dougal Glanville, Jan Glaser, Nick Gold, Michael Gordon, Martin Gore, Daniel Griffiths, Peter Grimsdale, John Hamilton, Rachael Hamilton, Hanningfield Metals, Bob Harding, Douglas Hart, Tess Hayles, Taka Hirose, Seth Hodder, Mathew Holland, Stewart Homan, Seiji Horibe, Michael Hutchence, Pascale Hutton, Andrew Innes, Jesse Ismail, Mamiko Itai, Pepe Jansz, David Johannsen, Rosko John, Michael Karoli, Darius Keeler, Trish Keenan, Simon Keep, Kim Kennedy, Jonathan Kessler, Deirdra Kimbell, Noriko Kitago, Yvette Lacy, Barnaby Laws, John Leahy, Jon Lee, Jaki Liebezeit, Owen Lodge, Don Ludlow, Tim Lund, Joanna MacGregor, Andrew Macintosh, Dave Marsh, Matheu Martin, Paul Martin, Moira Maxwell, Hamish McAlpine, Nicola Meighan, Daniel Miller, Rob Mitchell, Julian Moray, Grant Nicholas, Kate Nielsen, Alex Nightingale, Jack Notman, Nicky O'Donnell, Martin Orpen, Scott Parker, Alan Parks, Kirk Pengeley, Gilles Peterson, Francis Pickering, Martin Pike, Gerry Pilgrim, Rachel Pilkington, Production Response, Michael Proudfoot, Simon Quance, Fanja Ralison, Elliot Rashman, Keith Reilly, Mat Robin, Mathew Rudd, Laetitia Sadier, Phil Sasada, Ron Scalpello, Hildegard Schmidt, Irmin Schmidt, Eddie Scott, Annabelle Scott-Curry, Hepzibah Sessa, Dave Shaw, Talvin Singh, Roni Size, Luke Slater, David Smith, Nikki Smith, Dom Sotgio, Stansted Airport Fire Department, Roj Stevens, Iain Stewart, Freddie Stopler, Angie Somerside, SVC, Paul Taylor, Nicole Towler, Patrick Uden, David van der Gaag, John L. Walters, Tim Walton, Clare Ward, Mike Watson, Jason West, Tess Wight, Alan Wilder, Paris Wilder, Michael Williams, Steve Wilsher, Tony H. Wilson, Sarah Withers, Suzanne Wooder, Dave Yori and Zanna.

Editor:
Adrian Shaughnessy

Book designers:
Mat Cook
Julian House
Adrian Talbot

Moving image:
Julian Gibbs
K8 Dawkins

Business affairs:
Katy Richardson

Co-ordination:
Sarah Barlow

Introduction:
John O'Reilly

Intro:
Sarah Barlow
Mat Cook
Yaw Dako
Charlotte Dale
K8 Dawkins
Simon Dovar
Nima Falatoori
Lee Fasciani
Julian Gibbs
Dominic Goldberg
Kirsteen Haxton
Lisa Hetherington
Richard Higgins
Nikki Hildesley
Steph Hollinshead
Julian House
Dena Johnson
Wilf Johnston
Matthew Jones
Martina Keller
Oliver Laugsch
Georgina Lee
Roland Levy
Elaine Macintosh
Sonia Makkar
Sunita Panday
Katy Richardson
Melissa Robertson
Kate Rogers
Chris Sayer
Adrian Shaughnessy
Adrian Talbot
Rav Vythelingum
Ulrich Whyte

Intro
35 Little Russell Street
London WC1A 2HH
T +44 20 7637 1231
F +44 20 7636 5015
www.introwebsite.com

Published in 2001
by Laurence King Publishing
71 Great Russell Street
London WC1B 3BP
T +44 20 7430 8850
F +44 20 7430 8880
E enquiries@laurenceking.co.uk
www.laurenceking.co.uk

Text and design © Intro 2001

A catalogue record for this book
is available from the British Library.

ISBN 1 85669 274 4   333098
                      741.6 DIS

Printed in Hong Kong